Stories My Mother Never Told Me

STORIES

...my mother never told me

(*and some my teacher didn't either*)

STEVEN R. BUTLER

Poor Scholar Publications
Richardson, Texas

Poor Scholar Publications

Cover Illustration:
"Westward the Course of Empire Takes Its Way"
By Emmanuel Leutze
U.S. Capitol, Washington, D.C.

All portions of this book that are not in the public domain are copyright © 2021 by Steven R. Butler, unless otherwise indicated. All rights reserved.

FIRST EDITION

ISBN 978-0-9981526-7-7

Portions of this book were originally published in *From London to Kentucky: The Life and Times of James Haycraft, Jr. and His Son, Samuel Haycraft, Sr.*, copyright © 2017 by Steven R. Butler

All quoted passages in this book are either from works that are in the public domain or asserted by the author to be in accordance with the "Fair Use" provision of U.S. copyright law.

Additional copies of this book are available from:
Amazon.com and other online stores

10 9 8 7 6 5 4 3 2 1

"If history were taught in the form of stories, it would never be forgotten."

—Rudyard Kipling.

Dedicated to the memory of my mother,
IDA LOUISE JENKINS BUTLER VICTORY PIRMAN
(1930-1995)

And also, three women who either directly or indirectly helped me discover some of these stories:

My aunt, EMMA INEZ JENKINS HICKMAN

My grand-aunt, MAUDE IRENE SEAY PRINCE

and

My first cousin 1x removed, JOYCE CALCOTE DREW

For all my family,
but especially
Benjie, Nathan, Noah, and Samuel

Contents

Introduction	ix
1: Captive in the Catskills	1
2: The Runaway Servant	27
3. Transported!	37
4: The Malevolent Magistrate	61
5: McIntosh's "Stepping Stone"	77
6. The Last Battle of the Revolution	105
7: A Daring Escape	127
8. A Blessing in Disguise	141
9: Connections to Lincoln	155
10 The Riot at Purdy	185
11: Uncle Jack and the U-Boat	203
12: The "Old Salt" and His Stories	215
Appendix I: Text of Runaway Servant Ad	243
Appendix II: Westsylvania Memorial	244

The author as a six-year-old boy at the Alamo, San Antonio, Texas, 1955.

Introduction

When I was nine years old and a student in Mrs. Diane Adair's fourth grade class at R. E. Good Elementary School in Carrollton, Texas, we had something called "show and tell," an assignment that required my classmates and I to bring some small item of interest to school on a designated day, and then at the direction of our teacher, each pupil, in turn, would stand up in front of the class to show whatever he or she had brought and tell a little bit about it, hence the term "show and tell." The item could be almost anything at all—a favorite toy, a favorite book, a photograph, a souvenir of some kind—it really didn't matter what, as long as it was relatively small and possibly interesting. Looking back, I realize now that though Mrs. Adair didn't characterize it as such, this was also a useful exercise in public speaking.

Now, I don't recall what my classmates thought of "show and tell." Some may have dreaded it, but I didn't. Truth be told, it was right up my alley. The year before, when I was in the third grade at Edwin J. Kiest Elementary in Dallas, my teacher, Mrs. La Juan Johnson, remarked: "Steven brings to class many interesting anecdotes and much historical background of famous people and places. How we enjoy these!"

As it happens, this interest in famous people and places began earlier, even before I started school, when in 1954 and 1955, animator Walt Disney produced not just one, but three one-hour-long episodes about American folk hero Davy Crockett for the "Frontier Land" segment of his "Disneyland" television program, which starred a fellow Texan, actor Fess Parker. From the moment I saw the first one, like almost every kid in America—black, white, brown, and boys and girls alike—I was bitten by the Davy Crockett bug and I couldn't get enough. I can't explain why, but you only have to look at photos of me at age five and six to see the phenomenon personified. I had a Davy Crockett coonskin cap, a Davy Crockett toy rifle, a Davy Crockett t-shirt, Davy Crockett comic books, Davy Crockett records, and just about everything I could talk my parents into buying me that had anything at all to do with Davy Crockett.

I also had a toy Alamo, complete with tiny soldiers, which I received as a birthday or Christmas present, and when my father took me to San Antonio to see the real Alamo in the summer of 1955, I was in my glory. Seeing the actual site where Davy had fought and died, just like Walt Disney portrayed it on TV, was one of the most exciting things that ever happened to me. It also made me realize that places like the Alamo, where history happened, weren't just words or pictures in a book. They were *real* places, where *real* people did all the *real* things we read about in books, or saw recreated in movies or television programs.

Introduction

In the more than sixty years since then, I've traveled all over the country, and overseas as well, going out of my way to visit the actual places where famous people lived, or fought, or died, and historic events transpired. I still think it's one of the best ways to bring the past to life.

Something else has also helped bring the past to life for me: *Family history*. For that, I must credit my paternal grandmother, with whom I spent a lot of time when I was a boy. The weekend before my pending fourth grade "Show and Tell" assignment, I mentioned it to her, adding that I wasn't sure what to bring to school. To help, she loaned me a pair of cotton socks that she said her mother—my great-grandmother—had hand-knit for her father—my great-grandfather—when he was a soldier in the Civil War, and that's what I took to class.

Now, I wish I could tell you that my fellow students found my great-grandfather's socks pretty interesting, but truth be told, it was so long ago, I honestly can't remember. Maybe they did, maybe they didn't. However, I *am* certain about one thing: Though seemingly ordinary and insignificant, those socks not only brought history to life in my mind, the same as visiting the Alamo had done, they also made it *personal*. Knowing that my great-grandfather—a man I never met but to who I was related—had taken part in one of the most important events in American history—a war that I was only just then starting to learn about—while wearing a pair of hand-knit cotton socks that I could hold in my hand, look at, and even feel the texture, formed a link from him to me, while at the same time they likewise connected me to the big event in which he'd taken part. Looking back, I realize now that those socks were the spark that ignited my lifelong interest in family history.

However, as it happened, although I never lost my interest in history in general (it was my best subject in school, an "A" I could always count on earning), I really didn't think much more about my family's part in it until 1971, when I found a box of old photographs belonging to my grandmother (who was by this time living in a nursing home) in my father and stepmother's attic. When I looked at those pictures and realized that apart from my great-grandfather, I knew almost nothing about my ancestors—who they were, where they came from, and what they did with their lives, my interest in family history was reawakened, once again thanks to something belonging to my grandmother. Today, thanks also to a half-century of my own efforts, as well as some help from other people—most notably three of the four women to whom I've dedicated this book—I am far more knowledgeable than I was back then.

I'm also pleased to report that my family history research has resulted in a bonus I didn't expect when I first began it: My knowledge of history in general, and in particular the history of America, has likewise been enlarged, by leading me to learn some things about it that I never learned in school, *and I'm still learning today.*

Introduction

That last statement might surprise you. With three degrees in History (Bachelor's, Master's and Doctorate), you'd think I'd be so well informed on the subject that I couldn't possibly find anything "new" to learn, but the truth is that not a day goes by without my discovering something about history that I didn't know the day before, and interestingly, whatever it might be is almost always a result of my family history research, and nearly as often, it's something I never knew before because it wasn't taught or mentioned in school.

Which brings me to one of the main reasons why I wrote this book, namely to show how family history can be used to both learn about and teach history in general.

A little more than eighteen years ago, I became an adjunct professor at a nearby community college where I still teach courses in U.S. and Texas History. Somewhere along the line, in order to put some "life" into my lectures, I started illustrating my lessons, whenever it seemed appropriate, with the real-life experiences of some of my ancestors. I hoped it would help my students comprehend that the people who lived during the times they were learning about were not just words in a textbook or pictures on a PowerPoint slide, but real, live men and women who had to find ways to cope with the conditions of the era in which they found themselves. So far, student feedback has largely been positive, which is why I have continued the practice to this day.

I also began recommending that students watch one of my favorite TV programs: The popular PBS series "Finding Your Roots," hosted by Professor Henry Louis Gates, where a team of professional researchers use documentary evidence and DNA test results to help well-known contemporary figures—actors, musicians, artists, politicians, and so on—connect with their ancestors and, at the same time, learn something new about history as well. "The History Detectives" is another one of my favorites. In this show, four experienced researchers—two men and two women—help ordinary people, not celebrities, discover the significance of some historical object they've acquired, or help them find out if a family story connected to some inherited item, is true or not.

One of the reasons I like these shows so much is because in my case I can relate not only to the people seeking answers to their questions, but also to the individuals doing the research. Apparently, a lot of other people like these series too, and probably for another reason that I like them so much: Because almost every time I watch these programs, I learn something new about history that I never knew before. Some years ago, thinking about this led me to wonder if there might be a wider audience for my family history stories than my students (and also my relatives, of course, who I try to keep informed). Consequently, I began to contemplate writing this book, and also its forthcoming companion volume, *Stories My Father Never Told Me*. At

Introduction

long last, I have done so in the hope that book sales will prove that I was not just indulging in wishful thinking!

There's another reason I wrote this book: To inspire others to explore their own family's history, where they will almost certainly find their own stories, and then share them—if not in the classroom or a book, as I have done, then at least around the dinner table, or at family gatherings during the holiday season, or on some other appropriate occasion.

I encourage people to do this because I am mindful of something that I firmly believe is incumbent upon anyone who acquires such knowledge, *and that is to share what's learned*—not only with one's present-day family, but also future generations, so that the accumulated information does not become "lost" again, as it was or might have been before the search began. One way to do that is by writing a book like this one, even if not intended for publication.

Now, let me tell you something about the title of this book.

The main title of this book (and its companion volume) was inspired, in part, by the title of former President Barack Obama's autobiographical first book, *Dreams from my Father*. Mentioning this gives me the opportunity to point out something else I've learned through family history research: Although neither has ever invited the other to his home for Thanksgiving dinner (not yet, anyway), the 44th President and I are ninth cousins (once removed) by virtue of a common ancestor—a French immigrant named Mareen Duvall—on his mother's side of the family, and mine too!

Something else that the former Chief Executive and I have in common is that his book, like mine, is the result of both travel and personal inquiry. I recommend his book, by the way, if you have not already read it.

The title of my book is not a metaphor, however. It is literal truth. My mother never told me any of the stories this volume contains. Why not? *One good reason is that she did not know them herself.* Why didn't she know them? Because by the time she was born, these stories had become "lost" to her and her family, something akin to the way that artifacts and the ruins of structures sometimes become literally buried beneath the so-called "sands of time." In short, they weren't passed on. I have often wondered though, if she *had* known them, would she have shared them with me anyway? Truth be told, and I almost hate to say this, but my mother had practically no interest in or curiosity about her family's history, the result, no doubt, of a less-than-happy childhood. "Let the dead stay buried," she'd say, in sharp contrast to her older sister, my Aunt Nez, who when I turned to her for help, was both willing and eager to provide it.

The second part of the title, "And Some My Teacher Didn't Either," is likewise literally true. Almost every story in this book illuminates some facet of history that I never learned about in school, not because I wasn't paying attention—U.S. History and Western Civilization were two of the few courses in which I excelled in school—but because they are largely about things that weren't a part of the curriculum, or mentioned only briefly.

You see, the trouble with history, and this might sound strange coming from someone who can't seem to get enough of it, is that sometimes there's just too much, at least when it comes to the *teaching* of it. As I have often complained to my students (although they are in no position to do anything about it), when I was a freshman college student in 1972, American History was taught in two 3-credit-hour courses—U.S. History I, which went to the end of Reconstruction (1877), and U.S. History II, which covered from the end of Reconstruction to the present day. Nearly fifty years later, this is still the way U.S History is taught in colleges and universities, at least in the state of Texas and I don't doubt elsewhere. This poses a particular challenge for professors who are expected to cover the additional half century that's passed since 1972 because U.S. History II is still a 3-credit hour course. By rights, it should now be a 4-credit hour course, but it isn't. Bottom line: All that additional material can't be taught without the professor either stopping well short of the present day, or by leaving out some events. U.S. History I, which stops at the end of Reconstruction, is also problematic because today's teachers and professors are expected to teach additional material that wasn't part of the curriculum before the 1970s, when history books were enlarged to cover the role of women and minorities in American history. Now let me be clear: I have no problem whatever with that. In fact, I wholeheartedly agree it should be done, but unfortunately, state legislatures and state boards of education—the people who control these things—have not lengthened courses to provide the additional time needed. It's like trying to stuff one hundred pounds of potatoes into a fifty-pound sack. Like it or not, you're simply not going to be able to fit them all in. K-12 teachers have the same problem as college and university professors and this, I think, is the main reason why so many Americans know only the basic outline of their nation's history and nothing more—because the people who are charged with teaching it have little or no extra time to go into details, however interesting and informative they might be. The fault's not in the classroom though, it's in the state capitols. In a way, what History teachers and professors are expected to do is a lot like what's called an "unfunded mandate," which is something that's required by law, but the lawmakers won't give you what you need to make it happen. In education, It's not just funding that's in short supply. It's also time.

That being said, let me now tell you a little something about the dozen stories in this book.

All these stories are about topics or events in history with which I was either previously unacquainted or that I knew very little about until I discovered that one or more of my ancestors had taken part in them. With some few exceptions, I don't doubt that these topics and events are similarly unknown to most of my readers. Admittedly, a handful are of a personal nature, such as my recollections of an eccentric uncle, which aren't likely to be included in a standard History course, even if time allowed, but most of them *could* be, although my forebears' particular part in them may or may not be singled out for special attention by textbook authors.

As the title suggests, each one of the dozen stories in this book involves some ancestor of mine, either direct or collateral (like an aunt, or uncle, or cousin) on my mother's side of the family, just as *Stories my Father Never Told Me*, this book's companion volume, consists of stories that come only from my father's side.

Now, let's take a quick look at these tales.

First of all, three of these stories (which, by the way, are arranged in chronological order), are about some less-than-friendly close encounters with America's native people, popularly known, thanks to Christopher Columbus, as "Indians." All took place during the colonial period or the American Revolution, and each one—"Captive in the Catskills," "McIntosh's 'Stepping Stone,'" and "The Last Battle of the Revolution"—is a tale of survival. If they weren't, I could not have written about them for the simple reason that if any one of my ancestors had died as a result of these encounters, and before having children, obviously I wouldn't have been born!

Another group of three focus on events of the Civil War. One of the three goes even further, telling about a tragic incident that happened after the war, during Reconstruction. Two of the three—"A Daring Escape" and "A Soldier's Lucky Break"—are also tales of survival, in both cases against the odds. The third—"The Riot at Purdy"—is not.

The title of the next-to-last chapter—"Uncle Jack and the U-boat"—is about something that happened during the Second World War. What makes it unique is that it brings to light the way that Nazi Germany managed to bring the war to the United States, and also because it involves a branch of the armed forces that most people probably overlook when thinking of that particular conflict. Furthermore, it has an ending with a bit of a twist.

The remaining five stories are all about different things that happened at different times throughout our nation's history. One thing they have in common, apart from the fact that they involved one or more of my ancestors or relatives, is that what happened was something out-of-the-ordinary. For example, "Transported!" tells what occurred when one of my forebears, a poor London chimney sweep, decided one day to supplement his meager income by thievery. The title of "The Runaway Servant" is self-explanatory. Conversely, you wouldn't know from its title that "The Malevolent Magistrate" is about what happened when the daughter of one of my immigrant ancestors had a baby out of wedlock. "The Lincoln Connections," another self-

Introduction

revealing title, is actually four stories in one—a collection of tales telling how some of my ancestors had a link, however tenuous it might have been, to America's most highly esteemed president. Finally, there is "The 'Old Salt' and His Stories," which is about an uncle that I actually knew—an entertaining eccentric famed for his repertoire of tall tales as well as his peculiar behavior.

So, to reiterate: The purpose of this book is to demonstrate how family stories can not only enlarge a person's knowledge of history but also how they can be used to teach it, and hopefully, if I got it right, to entertain as well.

Now, it's time for you to see for yourself!

Steven R. Butler
April 2021

THE STORIES

THE CAPTIVE MOTHER AND BABE.

From Lossing's *Our Country: A Household History* (1879).

Captive in the Catskills

It has often occurred to me that if just one of my ancestors had failed to survive some sort of life-threatening situation before having a chance to reproduce, I would not be here to tell about it. The following story is the first of three examples I've chosen for this book. It concerns not just one, but *three* of my direct ancestors, who in 1663 experienced an ordeal it's unlikely they ever forgot.

****

If asked which nation led the way in colonizing the present-day eastern seaboard of the United States, most Americans would probably answer either "England" or "Great Britain," which is true of course, but that is not the whole story. Only seven years after a small band of English adventurers founded Jamestown, Virginia, and more than six years before the so-called "Pilgrims" beheld the shores of present-day Massachusetts, another group of Europeans arrived to colonize the region that lay in-between those two places, a vast expanse that would one day include the United States' largest and most important city: New York.

Although the Dutch West India Company established this colony (in 1614) and named it *Nieuw Nederlandt*, not all its inhabitants were Dutch. A great many, including several of the colony's first settlers, were actually *Walloons*, a religious and ethnic group that originally came from the Spanish Netherlands, a region encompassing present-day Belgium, Luxembourg, and a fair-sized portion of northern France.

For decades Spain had also ruled over the present-day Netherlands (or Holland, as it is more popularly known) but in 1581, following a lengthy war for independence, the Dutch people, who were mainly Calvinist Protestants, not only overthrew their Spanish master, King Philip IV, but also established a republic—a loose confederation of seven "United Provinces," also known as the "United States." This was in an age when monarchies were the norm and republics uncommon. But the Protestant Walloons, a Celtic people who resided in a land where their religious beliefs, combined with their unique way of "speaking French that was even then quaint and old in its forms," made them "a class sharply distinct from the mass of the people." As a result, they were "a marked race, out of place among the Flemish [and largely Roman Catholic] subjects of [King] Philip [of Spain]" and subject, not surprisingly, to religious persecution.[1]

---

[1] William Cullen Bryant and Sydney "Howard Gay, *A Popular History of the United States, Volume I* (New York: Scribner, Armstrong, and Company, 1876), 365.

Equally unsurprising, many Walloons left the Spanish Netherlands, to seek a religious haven in the United Provinces. Later, others found freedom of conscience in a part of southern Germany called the *Palatinate*, where European Protestants were also permitted to live and worship in safety in cities such as Frankenthal and Mannheim.

One of these later refugees, wrote historian Charles W. Baird, was a Walloon named Louis Du Bois, "a son of Chrétien Du Bois," who was born on October 27, 1626 or 1627 at Wicres, a small village located in the district of La Barrée, near Lille, in the Artois region of Flanders.[2] Although the place of his birth is now within the boundaries of France, in the 1620s it was still a part of the Spanish Netherlands. By the time he reached adulthood, however, Du Bois had left the land of his birth and along with "many [other] French refugees" had taken up residence in the city of Mannheim.[3]

It was there, on October 10, 1655, at the age of about twenty-eight, that Louis Du Bois married Catharine, a daughter of Mathése (or Matthew) Blanchan, "a burgher of that place" Because the Blanchan family also came from

---

[2] Charles W. Baird, *History of the Huguenot Emigration to America* (New York: Dodd, Mead & Company, Publishers, 1885), 187; Koehler, Sara Martin, *Huguenot Ancestors Represented in the Membership of the Huguenot Society of New Jersey*, 2nd edition (Bloomfield, New Jersey?: Huguenot Society of New Jersey, 1956), 29; Ralph Le Fevre, *History of New Paltz, New York and Its Old Families, From 1678 to 1820* (Albany, New York: Fort Orange Press, 1909), 6. It is Baird who gives 1627 as the year of Louis Du Bois' birth; others give 1626. We do not know which is correct.

[3] Ibid., 187-188; Le Fevre, 6.

Artois, it may be that the two young people had known each other before arriving in the Palatinate.[4] In any case, it is believed that Catharine was about twenty years of age at the time, having been born about 1635.[5] It turned out to be a fruitful partnership. Within four years of their wedding, Catherine gave birth, at Mannheim, to two sons whose names were almost certainly inspired by the Old Testament of the Bible: Abraham, born 1657, and Isaac, born about 1659.[6]

Although Louis and Catherine had no apparent reason to leave a place where people were "encouraged in the free exercise of their religion," living so close to "the border of France, and liable to foreign invasion at any moment," may have made them uneasy. Within a few years of their marriage, Louis and Catherine Du Bois "and certain of [their] fellow-refugees determined to remove to the New World."[7]

It is also possible, and perhaps even more likely, that these Walloons were motivated by economic factors. From the very earliest days of *Nieuw Nederlandt*, the Dutch West India Company, which controlled the colony with the permission of the States-General of the United Provinces, circulated pamphlets designed to encourage immigration by

---

[4] Baird, 188; Le Fevre, 6; Kohler, 29.
[5] Mike Judd, *Du Bois/Blanchon Family Page* (www.intercom.net/local/richardson/DuBois.html), accessed August 9, 1999.
[6] Le Fevre, 510.
[7] Baird, 188-189.

offering would-be colonists free land and other generous enticements.[8] One of these publications, issued in February 1661, proclaimed not only that "all Christian people of tender conscience" would be permitted to settle in *Nieuw Nederlandt* but also that the Dutch West India Company would grant each immigrant "fifteen leagues of land in breadth along the sea side and as far in depth in the Continent as any plantation hath or may be settled...with jurisdiction of all bayes and rivers comprehended within [its] bounds." Moreover, stated the circular, each colonist was assured "free propriety" of his land with full "power to dispose thereof for ever either by will contract bond or otherwise."[9]

If the offer of free land was not sufficient to tempt them, immigrants were also assured that "they and their associates" would be permitted to "establish their high, middle, and low jurisdiction; the better to maintain their authority," and that they would be "free of payinge head-money, for the space of twenty years." Other enticements for potential colonists included the right to keep any gold or silver they might find "with exemption of all dutyes and recognizances, for the tyme of twenty yeere and of other taxation for the tyme of tenne yeere." Ten years of exemption was also promised "for all such goods as shalbee

---

[8] Van der Zee, 42.
[9] John Romeyn Brodhead, ed., *Documents Relative to the Colonial History of the State of New York; procured in Holland, England and France*, vol. 3 (Albany, New York: Weed, Parsons and Company, Printers, 1858), 37-39.

transported into the said Colony for traffique with the Natives or otherwise" as well a ten-year exemption "for paying the Company their right of furrs, dyes, and any groth and all mechandize that shalbee exported." Immigrants who hoped to earn their living from the sea, rather than farming or engaging in the fur trade, were assured that they "may freely erect and establish within their colony the fishing trade and transport the same into Spaine the Streights or elsewhere, free from any recognition, during the terme of twenty yeere."[10]

Permission to choose their own "Director or Chiefe," should they find fault with the present Director-General of the colony or his replacement, was yet another right granted to the colonists.[11]

Although it appears that the Dutch West India Company lived up to its promises of free land, self-government, and freedom from taxes, it was somewhat less than forthcoming in its advertisement of the physical and geographic characteristics of the colony itself. That *Nieuw Nederlandt* laid "betweene 39 & 40 degrees" latitude was close enough to the truth and that it was "not above six weekes sayle from Holland" was equally accurate but the statement that it enjoyed "the best clymate in the whole world" was doubtless an exaggeration. So too was the declaration that "seed may bee thrown into the ground, except six weeks, all

---
[10] Ibid.
[11] Ibid.

the yere long."[12] Obviously, whoever wrote these words was either a bald-faced liar or had never experienced the long, cold winters that characterize this region of North America.

Doubtless, there was some truth to the statement that there was "great profit [to] be made by fishing and "from traffique with the natives," particularly in the fur trade, but a description of *Nieuw Nederlandt's* native inhabitants as "a mild people" who only needed to "be drawne out of their blind ignorance to the saving light by Jesus Christ,"[13] could be disputed by any colonist whose person or property had fallen victim to the Indians when they went on the warpath.

Although Louis Du Bois and his family would eventually make the journey to North America, no doubt enticed by such circulars, Mathése Blanchan and his wife Madeline Jorisse, along with their three youngest children, as well as Catherine's sister Maria and her husband, Antoine Crispel, preceded them. In the spring of 1660, the two couples traveled from Mannheim to the Dutch republic, almost certainly by Rhine riverboat and possibly in company with other immigrants. On April 27, probably from Amsterdam, they set out across the Atlantic aboard the Dutch West India Company vessel, *De Vergulde Otter* (the "Gilded Otter"). In mid-June, following a six-week voyage, they arrived at *Nieuw Amsterdam*, the present-day city of New York.

---

[12] Ibid.
[13] Ibid.

Dutch West India Company pamphlet, *Freedoms, as Given by the Council of the Nineteen of the Chartered West India Company to All those who Want to Establish a Colony in New Netherland,* 1630. Courtesy Wikimedia Commons.

Landing of the Walloons; from Charles Carleton Coffin, *Old Times in the Colonies, Volume 1* (New York: Harper and Bros., 1880), 143.

On the passenger manifest, both Blanchan's and Crispel's occupation is given as "agriculturist," i.e., farmer. Not counting Capt. Cornelius Reyersz Vander Beets and his crew, the tiny vessel carried one-hundred-and-eleven persons including a contingent of fifteen Dutch soldiers, one of whom was married and had two children, and ninety-three immigrants, most of whom were Dutch or Walloon families. Two of the single passengers were Swedish.

Although they are not included on the passenger manifest, which is apparently incomplete, it is believed that

Louis Du Bois and his wife and two sons followed a little more than a year later aboard the ship *St. Jan Baptist*, arriving at *Nieuw Amsterdam* on August 6, 1661.[14]

Here is what New Amsterdam, "a quaint old town in...the middle of the seventeenth century," was like when they arrived:

New Amsterdam; from an old Dutch map; courtesy Library of Congress.

It was, in style, a reproduction of a Dutch village of that period, when modest brick mansions, with terraced gables fronting the street, were mingled with steep-roofed cottages with dormer windows in side and gables. It was then completely built. The area within the palisades was not large; settlers in abundance came; and for several years few ventured to dwell remote from the town, because of the hostile Indians, who swarmed in the surrounding forests. The toleration that had made Holland an asylum for the oppressed, was practised here to its fullest extent. "Do you wish to buy a lot, build a house, and become a citizen?" was the usual question put to a stranger. His affirmative answer, with proofs of sincerity, was a sufficient passport. They pryed not into private opinion or belief; and bigotry could not take root and flourish in a soil so inimical to its growth. The inhabitants were industrious, thrifty, simple in manners and living, hospitable, neighborly, and honest, and all enjoyed as full a share of human happiness as a mild despotism would allow.[15]

---

[14] Le Fevre, 6-7; Baird, 189; Carl Boyer, ed., *Ship Passenger Lists, New York and New Jersey, 1600-1825* (Newhall, California: Carl Boyer, 1978), 125 and 138; E. B. O'Callaghan, ed., *The Documentary History of the State of New York*, vol. III (Albany: Weed, Parsons & Co., Public Printers, 1850), 57.

[15] Benson J. Lossing, *The Hudson, from the Wilderness to the Sea* (New York: Virtue and Vorston,

Dutch family scene; from *A school history of the United States, from the discovery of America to the year 1878* (New York: Harper & Bros., 1879), 106.

The Blanchan and Crispel families apparently did not remain long in New Amsterdam, however. By December 7, 1660, they had reached the village of Esopus, a small settlement on the west bank of the Hudson River, slightly more than a hundred miles north of New Amsterdam. There, Dominie Blom, minister to the Dutch Reformed Church at that place, noted "their presence at his first celebration of

---

1866), 427.

the Lord's Supper."[16] Not surprisingly, Louis and Catharine Du Bois and their two sons also settled in Esopus, following their landing in the New Netherlands a few months later.

In 1652, an Englishman named Thomas Chambers founded the original Esopus community, which was apparently nothing more than a collection of neighboring farms. Between that time and the arrival of my Walloon ancestors, the settlement had been raided several times by Indians. In 1658, upon the advice of Dutch Governor Peter Stuyvesant, the settlers, "sixty or seventy in number," built a new town that was fortified against Indian attacks. Unfortunately, this did not deter the Indians. "Another outbreak of Indian ferocity," writes Baird, "stimulated by the white man's "fire-water and provoked by the brutality of some of the Dutch themselves—occurred in the following year, when a band of several hundred Indian warriors invested the little town for three weeks." Fortunately, a few months before the Blanchan, Crispel, and Du Bois families arrived, Governor Stuyvesant had managed to make peace and put an end to the "Great Esopus War, which," Baird relates, "for many months past, had convulsed all the settlements, from Long Island to Fort Orange, with fear."[17]

In 1661, the village of Esopus was re-named Wiltwyck and it is Baird, once again, to whom we turn for a

---
[16] Le Fevre, 509.
[17] Baird, 191-192.

description of what the place must have looked like to recently arrived immigrants:

> [The village] lay but a short distance from that noble river [the Hudson], whose majestic course and varied scenery must have vividly recalled to them the Rhine. The plateau upon which the village of Wiltwyck stood was skirted by Esopus Creek. From the banks of along which the palisades protecting it had been constructed, the settlers overlooked the fertile lands occupied by the farms of the white men, and by the patches upon which the Indian women still raised their crops of maize and beans. The beautiful valley of the Wallkill opened toward the southwest. On the north, the wooded slopes of the Catskill mountains were visible.[18]

Baird also notes that around this time, yet another fortified town was built in the area. At first the settlers simply called it "Nieuw Dorp" ("the New Village"). Later, they renamed it Hurley. It was here, not long after their arrival at Wiltwyck, that Louis Du Bois, his father-in-law, Mathése Blanchan, and his brother-in-law Antoine Crispel moved their families.[19]

Unfortunately, the peace that Peter Stuyvesant had earlier negotiated with the Indians of the Esopus region was not long lasting. The Indians resented Stuyvesant for sending some Indian prisoners to the Dutch island of Curacao, in the Caribbean. "An additional grievance," apparently, was the settlers building the "New Village" on

---
[18] Ibid., 193.
[19] Ibid., 194.

land that the Indians still claimed. Again, we turn to Baird, to tell us what happened at Hurley and Wiltwyck, in the late spring and summer of 1663:

> Underrating either the courage or the strength of their wild neighbors, the settlers took no precautions against attack, but on the contrary, with strange infatuation, sold to them freely the rum that took away their reason and intensified their worst passions. The time came for an uprising. Stuyvesant had sent word to the Indian chiefs, through the magistrate of Wiltwyck, that he would shortly visit them, to make them presents, and to renew the peace concluded the year before. The message was received with professions of friendliness. Two days after, about noon, on the seventh of June, parties of Indians made a concerted attack upon both the settlements. The destruction of the "New Village" was complete. Every dwelling was burned. The greater number of the adult inhabitants had gone forth that day as usual to their fieldwork upon the outlying farms, leaving some of the women, with the little children, at home. Three of the men, who had doubtless returned to protect them, were killed; and eight women, with twenty-six children, were taken prisoners. Among these were the families of our Walloons: the wife and three children of Louis Du Bois, the two children of Matthew Blanchan, and Anthony Crispel's wife and child. The rest of the people, those at work in the fields, and those who could escape from the village, fled to the neighboring woods, and in the course of the afternoon made their way to Wiltwyck, or to the redoubt at the mouth of Esopus creek.[20]

Baird also tells us that the Indians were less successful in their attack on Wiltwyck, although they managed to burn

---

[20] Ibid., 194-195.

twelve houses and take several more women and children into captivity, for a total of forty-five from both towns.[21]

Seven members of the court at Wiltwyck, in a letter to the Council of New Netherland, provided a more detailed account of the attack on their town in their official report, dated June 20, 1663. A portion of the report reads:

> [The Indians] surprized [sic] and attacked us between the hours of 11 and 12 o'clock in the forenoon on Thursday the 7th Instant Entering in bands through all the gates, they divided and scattering themselves among all the houses and dwellings in a friendly manner, having with them a little maize and some few beans to sell to our Inhabitants, by which means they kept them within their houses, and thus went from place to place as spies to discover our strength in men. And after they had been about a short quarter of an hour within this place, some people on horseback rushed through the Mill gate from the New Village, crying out — "The Indians have destroyed the New Village!" And with these words, the Indians her in this Village [Wiltwyck] immediately fired a shot and made a general attack on our village from the rear, murdering our people in their houses, with their axes and tomahawks, and firing upon them with guns and pistols; they seized whatever women and children they could catch, and carried them prisoners outside the gates, plundered the houses and set the village on fire to windward, it blowing at the time from the South. The remaining Indians commanded all the streets, firing from the corner houses, which they occupied and through the curtains outside along the highways, so that some of our Inhabitants, on their way to their houses to get their arms, were wounded and slain. When the flames were at their height the wind changed to the west, were

---

[21] Ibid.

it not for which the fire would have been much more destructive. So rapidly and silently did Murder do his work that those in different parts of the village were not aware of it until those who had been wounded happened to meet each other, in which way the most of the others also had warning. The greater portion of our men were abroad at their field labors, and but few in the village.[22]

A small number of male villagers, some armed, some not, the report added, had managed to come running and put the Indians "to flight." "After these few men had been collected against the Barbarians," the burghers continued, "by degrees the others arrived, who as it has been stated, were abroad at their field labors, and we found ourselves when mustered in the evening, including those from the new village, who took refuge amongst us, in number 69 efficient men, both qualified and unqualified." Their first task, the report revealed, was to immediately replace "the burnt palisades…by new ones." That night, "the people [were] distributed…along the bastions and curtains to keep watch."[23]

A month passed before Governor Stuyvesant was able to gather and send a force of English and Dutch soldiers, under the command of Captain Martin Kregier, "for the defense of Wiltwyck, and for the rescue of the prisoners in the hands of the Esopus Indians." Meanwhile, the people of

---

[22] E. B. O'Callaghan, ed. *The Documentary History of the State of New York*, vol. iv (Albany: Charles Van Benthuysen, Public Printer, 1851), 29.
[23] Ibid., 30.

the two settlements rebuilt their fortifications and buried their dead, twenty-four in all. When one of the captured women, Rachel de la Montagne, managed to escape, she offered "to conduct the rescuing party to the Indian fort, thirty miles to the south-west of Wiltwyck, wither the prisoners had been conveyed."[24]

On July 27, 1663, Kregier and his men set out. "Tradition," says Baird, tells us that Louis Du Bois "was one of the foremost members of the rescuing party." Unfortunately, by the time they reached the spot where the captives had first been taken, "the Indians had retreated…to a more distant fastness in the Shawungunk mountains. The soldiers, writes Baird, "pursued them, but without success, and after setting fire to the fort, and destroying large quantities of corn which they found stored away in pits, or growing in the fields, the party returned to Wiltwyck." Yet another month passed before some friendly Indians told the soldiers about the location of a new fort the Esopus Indians had built. Writes Baird:

> So soon as the weather permitted, and a supply of horses could be obtained, Krygier set forth again. This time, the enemy was taken by surprise. A fierce combat ensued; many of the savages were taken, and twenty-three of the captives were recovered and brought back in triumph to the settlement. Their absence had lasted just three months. Tradition represents the pious Walloons as cheering the tedious hours of their bondage

---

[24] Baird, 197.

with Marot's psalms. When rescued by their friends, just as the savages were about to slaughter them, they were entertaining their captors, and obtaining a momentary reprieve, by singing the one hundred and thirty-seventh psalm: "By the rivers of Babylon, there we sat down, yea, we wept, when we remembered Zion…For there they that carried us away captive required of us a song."[25]

Another version of the rescue credits Catharine Du Bois, Louis' wife, with being the prisoner who sang psalms:

> About ten. weeks after the capture the Indians decided to celebrate their escape from pursuit by burning one of their captives. For their victim they selected Catharine du Bois and her baby, Sara, who afterward married Joost Janse Van Meteren. A cubical pile of logs was arranged and the mother and child were placed upon it; when the Indians were about to apply the torch, Catharine began to sing a Huguenot hymn she had learned in earlier days in France. The Indians withheld the fire and listened. When she finished they demanded another song and then another. Before the last hymn was finished Dutch Soldiers arrived, the captives were all rescued and the Indians terribly punished.[26]

This story, "which is dear to the Huguenot heart of New Paltz (a town that Louis Du Bois later helped to found)," writes Le Fevre, also includes "Louis Du Bois himself killing with his sword an Indian who was in advance of the rest before the alarm could be raised." The death of the Indian, "no doubt a scout…[who] had fallen asleep," it is

---

[25] Ibid., 197-198.
[26] Samuel Gordon Smyth, *A Genealogy of the Duke-Shepard-Van Metre Family* (Lancaster. Pennsylvania: The New Era Printing Company, 1909), 24.

said, "prevented the news of the approach of the white men being given to their savage foes." The intrepid Walloon is said to have also encountered an Indian woman named Basha, "who had gone to the spring a short distance north of the fort for water." When she attempted to alarm the warriors, "Louis Du Bois shot her with his gun and she fell in the spring, which still bears her name."[27]

As Le Fevre points out, Kregier's report contained none of these details. "However," he writes, "we shall not give up the tradition as it contains nothing irreconcilable with the report…which deals mainly with the fighting done by his soldiers, while tradition would dwell more upon the condition of the captives."[28]

Here, for the record, is Captain Martin Kregier's account of the rescue, dated September 5, 1663:

> Set out again day break, and about noon came to their first maize field where we discovered two Squaws and a Dutch woman; who had come that morning from their new fort to get corn. But as the creek lay between us and the corn-field, though we would fain have the women it was impossible to ford the stream without being seen and then discovered. We therefore, adopted the resolution to avoid the cornfield and the road, and turned in through the woods so as not to be seen. Arrived about two o'clock in the afternoon within sight of their fort, which we discovered situate[d] on a lofty plain. Divided our force in two —Lieutenant Couwenhoven and I led the right wing, and Lieutenant Stilwil and Ensign Niessen the left wing. Proceeded

---

[27] Le Fevre, 9.
[28] Ibid., 7.

in this disposition along the hill so as not to be seen and in order to come right under the fort; but as it was somewhat level on the left side of the fort and the soldiers were seen by a Squaw, who was piling wood there and who sent forth a terrible scream which was heard by the Indians who were standing and working near the fort, we instantly fell upon them. The Indians rushed forthwith through the fort towards their houses, which stood about a stone's throw from the fort, in order to secure their arms, and thus hastily picked up a few guns and bows and arrows, but we were so hot at their heels that they were forced to leave many of them behind. We kept up a sharp fire on them and pursued them so closely that they leaped into the creek, which ran in front of the lower part of their maize land. On reaching the opposite side of the Kill, they courageously returned our fire, which we sent back, so that we were obliged to send a party across to dislodge them. In this attack, the Indians lost their Chief, named Papequanaehen, fourteen other warriors, four women and three children, whom we saw lying both on this and on the other side of the creek but probably many more were wounded; when rushing from the fort to the houses, when we did give them a brave charge. On our side three were killed and six wounded and we have recovered three and twenty Christian prisoners out of their hands. We have also taken thirteen of them prisoners, both men and women, besides an old man who accompanied us about half an hour but would not go farther. We took him aside and gave him his last meal.[29]

Kregier reported that he and his men afterward cut down the Indian's maize, destroyed any weapons they found, and burned the fort. Before returning to Wiltwyck, they also took a great deal of booty, including deerskins, gun powder, and wampum belts.

---

[29]. O'Callaghan, *The Documentary History of the State of New York*, vol. iv, 47-48.

A Dutch soldier of the 17th Century; from De Gheyn's *Exercise of Armes* (1619).

Although the story about Catharine Du Bois singing psalms prior to nearly being burnt alive at the stake by her captors is a colorful one, at least one historian, E. M. Ruttenber, has given it little credence. He says:

> The story was repudiated as a statement of fact, first on the authority of Indian customs. We do not recall a single instance where a woman was burned at the stake by the Indians. They killed female prisoners on the march sometimes, when they were too feeble to keep up, but very rarely indeed after reaching camp.—Mrs. DuBois and her companions had been prisoners from June 19th to September 5, or nearly three months before they were rescued from captivity. During all that time they had been guarded carefully at the castle [fort] of the Indians, and held for ransom or exchange, to which end negotiations had been opened, the Indians asking especially the return of some of their chiefs who had been sent to Curaçao and sold as slaves by Governor Stuyvesant.
>
> Second: documentary evidence concerning the events of that period is entirely against the tradition. The written record is, that when the Dutch forces surprised the Indians, the latter were busy in constructing a third angle to their fort for the purpose of strengthening it, instead of being engaged in preparations for burning prisoners. (See Kregier's Journal.) The prisoners were found alive and well, and no complaint is recorded of any ill treatment, not even that their heads had been shaved and painted, as had been customary. Every night, says the record, they were removed from the castle to woods, lest the Dutch should recover them before negotiations for their release were consummated. The entire drift of the record narrative is against even the probability that an intention to burn, much more so of preparation to do so.[30]

---

[30] Le Fevre, 8.

Although Ruttenber himself made an error—the women and children were captured on June 7, not June 19—I believe he is probably correct in saying that the tradition is without any basis in fact, or if not a complete fabrication, it may be embellishment. Perhaps the women did sing psalms to comfort themselves while in captivity. Baird's account also includes an error: Sarah Du Bois, supposedly taken captive with her mother, was not born until 1664, the year following this incident. We also know, from Kregier's account, that only three Du Bois children were captured. These would have been six-year-old Abraham, four-year-old Isaac, and Jacob, nearly two years of age, the first member of his family born in America.

"These troubles over," Baird tells us, "the settlement enjoyed security from savage molestation." This was due in part, he tells us, to the near extermination of the Esopus tribe. This permitted the settlers to "extend their plantations further into the rich lands that were now without an owner." We also learn from Baird and others that in 1677, Louis Du Bois, "with several associates, removed from Wiltwyck to a spot they had discovered during their pursuit of the Indians." It was here, "in the beautiful Wallkill valley," that they "built their homes, near the base of the Shawungunk mountains." In honor of their former home on the Rhine, "and the days of their exile in Mannheim," they called the new settlement "le nouveau Palatinat" or "New Paltz," a town that still exists to this day.[31] We also know that the original deed to this land, granted by Governor Andros, is preserved at New Paltz.[32]

On March 27, 1694, nearly thirty-four years after coming to America and making his home in the Hudson River Valley of New York, Louis Du Bois wrote a will in which he named as heirs his wife Catrina (Catharine), sons Abraham, Jacob, David, Solomon, Louys, and Matthew, the children of his deceased son Isaac, and his daughter Sarah—who in 1682 had married Joost Jans Van Meteren (who as a boy had been carried into captivity by the Indians, along with his mother). A year or two later, he revoked the earlier will, making a different disposition of his estate. The will mentions a farm at Hurley and a lot in Kings[ton?], and land in New Paltz. Sometime after this, Louis died. The will was proved in court on March 26, 1696, and on July 16, 1697, his widow, Catrina (Catharine) was sworn in as executrix. Unfortunately, we do not know when she died.[33]

****

---

[31] Baird, 199.
[32] Sara Morton Koehler, ed., *Huguenot Ancestors Represented in the Membership of the Huguenot Society of New Jersey*, second edition (Bloomfield, New Jersey: Huguenot Society of New Jersey, 1956), 29.
[33] Berthold Fernow, *Calendar of Wills, On File and Recorded in the Offices of the Clerk of the Court of Appeals, of the County Clerk at Albany...* (Baltimore: Printed for the Clearfield Company by Genealogical Publishing Co., 1967), 98.

In August, 2000, while on a road trip to the Northeastern United States, my wife and I went out of our way to visit Kingston, New York—the former Wyldwick or Esopus—where I saw for myself the grave of my 9th great-grandfather, Louis Dubois, in the old Dutch churchyard that lies within the bounds of the original palisaded village where two of my ninth great-grandmothers, Catherine Blanchan Dubois and Macyken Hendrygksen Van Meteren, along with my eighth great-grandfather and Macyken's son, Joost Jans Van Meteren (then only three-years-old), had been taken captive by the Indians and carried off into the Catskill Mountains in 1663. During that visit, or perhaps sometime a little before or after, it occurred to me that if Catherine—who in 1664 gave birth to a daughter, Sarah, who would later become Joost Jans's wife—had died in captivity, I would never have been born. Likewise, if Joost Jans had died. In short, my very existence was dependent upon their survival. All I can say is "Thanks Captain Kregier!"

A Colonial tanner at work; from *The Book of Trades* (1806).

The Runaway Servant

If, like me, all or most of your ancestors came to America before the Revolution, and especially if they immigrated to one of the southern colonies, chances are that one or more of them arrived in the "New World" as something called an "indentured servant."

During most of the seventeenth century, before African slavery became firmly entrenched in America as the principal form of manual labor, indentured servants—contract laborers from the British Isles and elsewhere—did most of the work in the cash crop fields of Maryland, Virginia, the Carolinas, and Georgia, and though the number of indentured servants declined after African slavery took root, they never disappeared altogether.

In general, enslaved blacks and white indentured servants were treated the same, with every aspect of their lives controlled by their master. They were also subject to the same sorts of punishment, including whipping. However, unlike slaves, who were considered property and doomed to spend their entire lives working without pay for someone else, indentured servants eventually gained their freedom, usually after seven years. It should come as no surprise that sometimes slaves ran away, and probably, most Americans who take a U.S. History course are taught about that. But did you know that rather than wait for the term of their indenture to expire, so did many white servants. Why? Because they had an advantage. Unlike slaves, whose dark skin made them stand out in a population that was largely white, and thus more easily detected by authorities on the lookout for runaways, indentured servants could blend into nearly any community and if a white runaway could get far enough away from his or her master, the chances of remaining free, especially if he or she changed his or her name, were greatly improved. This next story is about of one of my ancestors who did just that!

****

In or about 1749, my fifth great-grandfather, Peter Danzer (or Dantzer), who later "Anglicized" his surname to Dancer, left his home in what is now the Federal Republic of Germany and traveled aboard a sailing ship to Savannah, Georgia, where upon arrival, he became an indentured servant to Messrs. William Spencer and Samuel Mercer. He was born so far as I know, about the year 1730, which means he was nineteen or twenty years old at the time he arrived in America. Nothing is known of his parentage, nor precisely where he came from, although the presence of a colony of Salzburgers in Georgia at this time lends weight to the supposition that he likewise came from Salzburg.

Some researchers claim, although Peter's name does not appear on the passenger manifest, that he made the transatlantic crossing aboard the brig *Charlestown Galley*, Captain Peter Bogg, which arrived at Savannah on October 2, 1749. This could be true, but there's no evidence of it.

Samuel Mercer, one of the two men to whom Peter owed seven years of labor, was a tanner by trade. Unsurprisingly, tanning leather was the job that Peter Dancer performed for him. Mercer was also one of the first settlers to arrive in the newly-established colony—the brainchild of English philanthropist James Oglethorpe—in 1733. In 1738 the colony's trustees appointed Mercer second constable of the fledgling city. Spencer, a vintner and a "gentleman," did not arrive until 1742. He too was an administrative official.

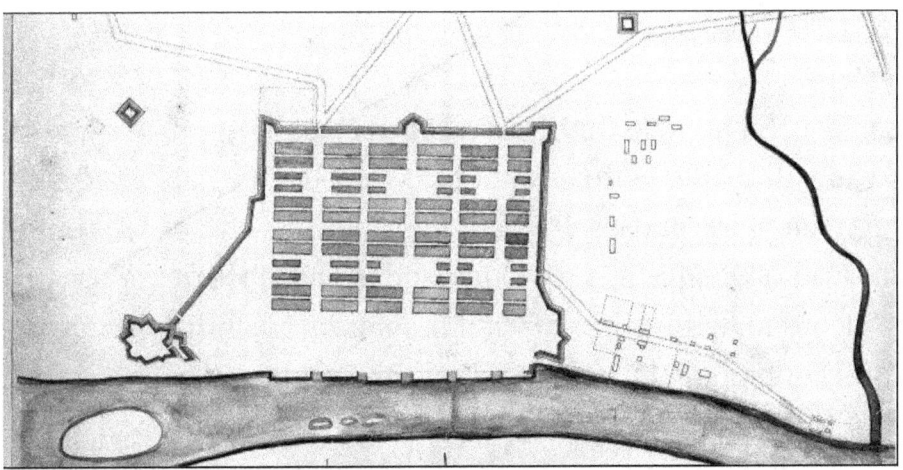

Savannah Georgia, as it was laid out in 1734; map courtesy Library of Congress, Washington, D.C.

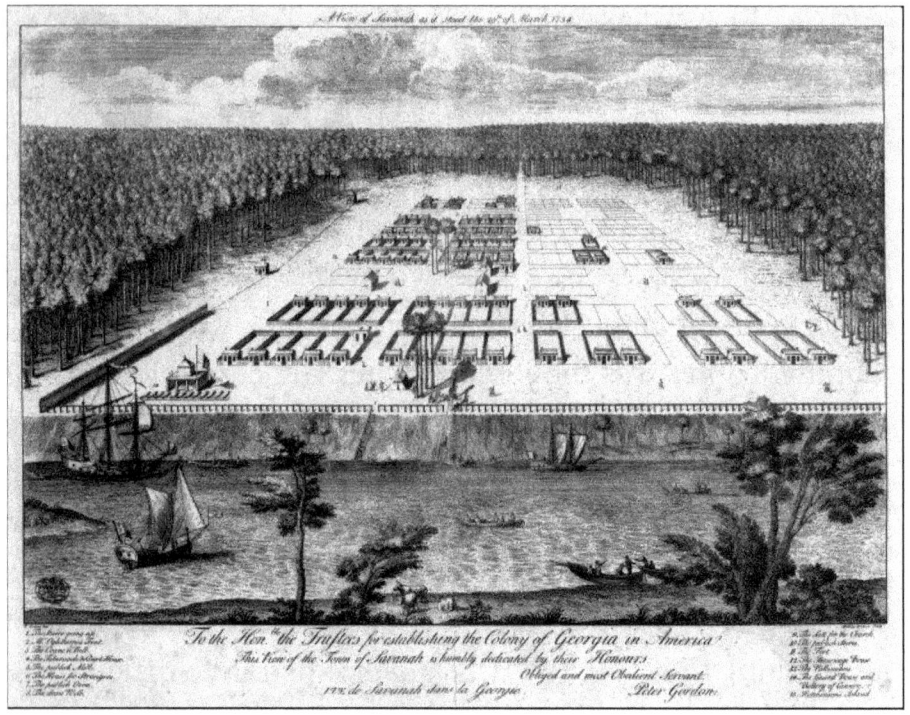

Savannah, 1734, about 15 years before Peter Dancer arrived; courtesy Library of Congress, Washington, D.C.

The Savannah that Peter Dantzer saw upon his arrival was still a city in the making, having been established only sixteen years earlier. Rectangular, with its streets laid out in a grid system, it was surrounded by fortifications that "afforded within its intrenchments an asylum whither the adjacent planters, upon occasions of alarm, might betake themselves with their families and personal property, and find refuge from the rifle and scalping-knife of the Indian." In each of the corner bastions "wooden towers were erected…with strong platforms in their first stories to support twelve pounder cannons."[1]

There's no known record of how Spencer and Mercer treated their servants, but apparently, Peter Dantzer did not like working for them, or maybe he just didn't like working in a tannery, because sometime in December 1749 or January 1750, only three months after his arrival in Georgia, he and three brothers who were likewise indentured servants—John Daniel Hertel, Henry Hertel, and John Broderick Hertel—ran away, crossing the Savannah River and escaping into the neighboring colony of South Carolina. Shortly afterward, the following notice appeared in the *South Carolina Gazette*:

> Whereas, John Daniel Hertel, aged 26 Years, by trade a butcher, a middle-sized man, pock-frettan, and wants a finger on one hand, Henry Hertel, aged 24 years, of the same trade, middle sized, of a fair complexion; John Broderick Hertel, aged 22 years, of the same trade, middle sized, a scar in his left cheek; and Peter Dantzer, aged 19, a tanner, of low stature and pock fretten; all indented servants to Messrs. William Spencer and Samuel Mercer of Savannah in the colony of Georgia, have lately run away from their said masters' Service and are Supposed to have Secreted themselves in that province. Whoever shall apprehend them or any of them, and, deliver them to the said William Spencer or Samuel Mercer, or to Mr. Robert N. Williams in [word illegible] shall receive the sum of TWENTY POUNDS current money of the province of South

---

[1] Charles C. Jones, *History of Savannah, Georgia* (Syracuse, New York: D. Mason & Co., 1890), 171-2.

Carolina for each one so taken and delivered, enclusive of all other reasonable charges for taking the same.[2]

I find this advertisement amusing because it not only mentions that the Hertel brothers were all butchers by trade, but also that John Daniel Hertel "wants a finger on one hand." I can't help but think that he wasn't a very careful butcher! It also puts me in mind of that old joke, "Did you hear about the butcher who backed into the meat grinder? *He got a little behind in his work!*"

Although all four young men were German, neither Peter Dantzer nor the Hertel brothers lived or worked among the Salzburgers who in 1734 had established a settlement called Ebenezer, about twenty-five miles upriver from Savannah. I am sure of that because not long after the four young men absconded, they were mentioned in a letter written by Mr. John Martin Bolzius, the religious leader of the German colony, to Mr. Martyn, Secretary of the colony, in which he complains of two servants running away from Ebenezer, followed almost immediately by "four servants at Savannah, viz. Peter Danzer & 3 brothers, Hertell by Name and Butchers by Trade." Bolzius went on to remark, "I am told, they are subsisted & encouraged likewise at the Congrees, the Refuge of all Sorts of People."[3] He also explained how difficult it was to apprehend runaways:

---

[2] *South Carolina Gazette*, Charles Town, South Carolina, January 22-29, 1750.
[3] *Colonial Records of the State of Georgia, Vol. 26* (Atlanta, Georgia: Franklin Printing), 80-83.

We had many more Deserters at Savannah & here (at Savannah attempting all to run away) but they were retaken and corrected a good deal less than they deserved. I am sure, they had no just Reason to complain of any hard usage in their respective Services, & having received so many Benefactions at London by the generous & paternal Care of the Honble. Trustees, it is very culpable & wicked in them, to break so shamefully their Contract signed freely & solemnly by them all. As long as such Things concerning the Servants don't come to a better Regulation in South Carolina; & as long as the Government there rather protects than returns our Deserters, we are obliged to deal very tenderly with ill-natured Servants to our great Disappointment & Losses, or else we must fear, they run away to Carolina & are allmost as safe as in St Augustine the Negroes. There is another Difficulty to apprehend Servants in Carolina, viz1 the general Indenture of the whole Embarkation of servants sent over by Their Honours. If a servant deserts our Place, we must copy the whole Indenture, & get it attested & sealed by the Magistrates at Savannah. Before this is done, the Servant escapes our on the other side of Savanah River. If each Servant had his own lawfull Indenture made out at London, & delivered here up to his Master, we could pursue him directly & prove our lawfull Claim to any Justice of Peace in South Carolina by producing such special Indenture.[4]

In all likelihood, Peter Dantzer and the Hertel brothers escaped into South Carolina by stealing or "borrowing" a boat and rowing or paddling across the Savannah River. I've crossed it myself, by car of course, using the Talmadge Memorial Bridge, which obviously didn't exist in 1750! As

---

[4] Ibid.

I did so, I couldn't help but think of my ancestor and wondered, what was he thinking when he crossed it, by boat, raft, or by swimming, more than two centuries earlier? Whether or not any one of the four young men was ever apprehended and returned to his masters is uncertain. If they hid out in the swampland along the Congaree River, or *Congrees* as Rev. Bolzius spelled it, it is entirely possible that all four managed to keep their freedom.

Although the fate of the Hertel brothers seems to be lost to history, I have every reason to believe that Peter Dancer, as he later styled himself, remained at large, and it's possible too that he did so without having to hide out in a swamp to avoid capture.

In 1733, by order of the Governor and Council of South Carolina, German Lutherans settled Saxe-Gotha Township (previously Congaree Township), a long strip of land on the southwest side of the Congaree River in what is now Lexington County, South Carolina. It's entirely possible (though unproven) that Peter Dancer, as well as the Hertel brothers, took refuge in this community after running away from their masters in Savannah. It would certainly make sense for them to want to be among people who spoke their language. The likelihood that this happened, insofar as Peter Dancer is concerned, is bolstered by evidence that he got married, had children, and eventually became a land owner in Richland County, South Carolina, which is on the opposite side of the Congaree River from Lexington County and is also where the state capital, Columbia, was established by an act of the legislature in 1786. Prior to that time, the capital of South Carolina was Charles Town, or simply "Charleston," as it is known today.

Unfortunately, the name of Peter's wife has also been lost to history, but I do know that the couple had at least three sons and two daughters. However, none of the Dancer children are identified by name in any available South Carolina records except the two oldest sons, Henry and John.

Two documents preserved in the South Carolina state archives reveal that in June 1770 Peter Dancer received a grant for 150 acres of land in Craven County, one of the three original colonial counties that were subdivided into smaller counties following independence from Great Britain. Other preserved documents show that in August 1771 he received a second grant, this time for an inverted T-shaped piece of land, containing 200 acres on the north side of the Broad River, a stream that connects with the Congaree River at the point where Columbia was established some fifteen years later. It is interesting to note that the present-day Congaree National Park, a preserved wilderness area that may or may not be the spot to which Peter Dancer and the Hertel brothers escaped in 1750, lies only seventeen miles south of present-day Columbia.

Unfortunately, although a plat of this second grant exists, it is difficult to tell, from either the boundary description or the crude map that accompanies it, precisely where this property was located, apart from it being "in Richland County," on the north side of the Broad River."

Peter Dancer died sometime in 1789, at the age of about fifty-nine. Although it appears that he did not leave a will, probate records for the then-new Richland County show that the job of administering his estate was given to his son Henry Dancer. An inventory of his property shows that he was not a wealthy man, having only some carpenter's tools, a cow and yearling, and 72 acres of land worth 36 Pounds. He had no slaves. Altogether, the total value of his estate came to 65 Pounds, 19 Shillings, and 5 Pence. What became of the other 228 acres he had received as grants in 1770 and 1771 is unknown, but presumably, by the time he passed away he had sold it.

****

In 2010, with my wife, I visited Columbia, South Carolina, which as I've pointed out is not far from where my ancestor lived. Unfortunately, at the time I did not have copies of the land grants he received, or I would have tried to find his property, although I'm not sure I would have succeeded. I would also have liked to visit his gravesite, to pay my respects, but also unfortunately, the location of that is presently unknown.

Transported!

Sometimes, family history research can lead you to things you never expected to find. As I mentioned in the book's Introduction, it can also lead you to learn some things about history that you never knew before. For instance, until I made the discovery that this story tells about, I thought that all the indentured servants who came to America during the colonial era, such as Peter Dantzer (or Dancer), who you read about in the preceding chapter, came over voluntarily, that is, of their own free will. As it happens, that was not always the case. Several years ago, while I was living and working in London, England, one of my co-workers—an Australian "bloke"—told me over a pint of English beer at a pub near our workplace that before the British government began sending convicts to penal colonies in the land "Down Under," petty criminals were "transported" to "His Majesty's Colonies and Dominions in North America." I was surprised. I had never heard of this before. None of my teachers ever mentioned it and it was absent from any history textbook that I had in either high school or college. Nevertheless, it's true. Some twenty years later, I was even more surprised when I discovered that I am descended from one of these immigrants-in-chains—in my case a London chimney sweep who with the help of three friends committed a burglary, was then locked up in London's notorious Newgate Prison, and finally, following a brief trial and verdict of "guilty," was sentenced to seven years "transportation" to Virginia! This is his story.

****

In his celebrated 1869 *History of Elizabethtown, Kentucky*, lifelong town clerk, Samuel Haycraft, Jr., included some biographical sketches of Hardin County's prominent early families. In regard to his own, Haycraft asserted that his grandfather, James Haycraft, Jr., was a seaman in the Royal navy who arrived in America about 1740, adding: "How he happened to stay, none living can now tell." Speculating that his emigrant ancestor either took "French leave" (i.e., deserted) or was discharged, he remarked that one way or the other he "liked the looks of the country and concluded to make it his own."[1] In 1878, this version of the family's New World origins was perpetuated in a sketch about James' son, Samuel Haycraft, Sr., which was published in *The Biographical Encyclopedia of Kentucky*.[2] However, this version is not accurate. Whether Samuel Haycraft, Jr. was truly ignorant of the

---

[1] James Haycraft, Jr., *A History of Elizabethtown, Kentucky and Its Surroundings* (Elizabethtown, Kentucky: The Women's Club of Elizabethtown, Ky., 1921), 120.
[2] J. M. Armstrong, *Biographical Encyclopedia of Kentucky of the Dead and Living Men of the Nineteenth Century* (Cincinnati, Ohio: 1878), 222.

actual circumstances that led to his English grandfather's arrival in America or was simply trying to protect his family's good name is uncertain. Whatever the case, it is a shame that he didn't know (or wouldn't tell) what really happened, for it is quite an interesting story.

It appears that James Haycraft, Jr. was born in London in 1719. In any event, the parish register of Saint Andrew's Church in Holborn records the christening of a child by that name on December 19th of that year. The infant's father was also named James Haycraft (or Haycroft as it was also spelled). His mother's given name was Hannah.[3] Her maiden surname is unknown. Although severely damaged by German bombs during World War II, Saint Andrew's, one of several London churches designed by Sir Christopher Wren, was rebuilt and I can personally attest to the fact that it is still standing to this day at Holborn Circus, EC1.

At about the time he reached adulthood (if we accept that he was the same person whose christening is recorded in the Saint Andrew's parish register), James Haycraft met a young woman named Ann Henley or Henry. Ann would later claim that she and James were married at the town of Malden, in Kent, about 1741.[4]

---

[3] St. Andrew's Holborn, Holborn Circus, City of London, Parish Register, Christenings, 1719: Guildhall Manuscripts Archive, London Metropolitan Archive, City of London, 40 Northampton Road, London EC1R 0HB, England, United Kingdom.

[4] Old Bailey Proceedings Online (www.oldbaileyonline.org), Version 6.0, 10 March 2012, May 1744, trial of James Haycraft, Ann Henley, otherwise Haycraft, Samuel Smytheman, Elizabeth Eaton (t17440510-9). See also Old Bailey Sessions Papers, 10 May 1744, 116-7 & 144, Guildhall Library

St. Andrew's Church, Holborn, London; author photo.

This is curious, most of all because there is no town Malden in Kent. There is however, a town called Maldon (spelled with an "o" instead of an "e") in Essex. Perhaps the court clerk made a mistake or possibly Ann misspoke. There is also the possibility that Ann lied and that the couple's

---

Manuscript Section, London Metropolitan Archives, City of London, 40 Northampton Road, London EC1R 0HB, England, United Kingdom., and Middlesex Sessions Rolls—Indictments 8th to 10th May 1744 (MJ/SR/2819), Folio 9, Middlesex Session Roll—Gaol Delivery (MJ/SR/2819), "A perfect calendar of all the prisoners committed to His Majesty's gaol Newgate from the 4thday of April 1744 to the 10th day of May 1744"; Middlesex Sessions Gaol Delivery Book—September 1736 to December 1745 (MJ?GBB/317), 150, London Metropolitan Archives, City of London, 40 Northampton Road, London EC1R 0HB, England, United Kingdom. NOTE: All subsequent references to this source material shall read "Ibid.," or "Old Bailey, see Note 4."

relationship was instead what is known as a "common-law" arrangement.

In any case, in 1744—during the reign of King George II—James Haycraft and Ann Henley were living together as man and wife in Saint Margaret's Parish, Westminster, in a dwelling located in Angel Court, Story's Gate,[5] close by Westminster Abbey. Modern day visitors to London will find that Angel Court no longer exists, but Story's Gate still leads to the southeast corner of Saint James' Park, just as it did in the mid-eighteenth century. Saint Margaret's Church also still stands, immediately adjacent to Westminster Abbey, and not far from where the two young people resided.

At this time, James Haycraft made his living as a chimney sweep. A fellow sweep, whose name was Samuel Smytheman, lived in nearby Petty France street with a young woman named Elizabeth Eaton. From all accounts, Haycraft and Smytheman met in late 1743 or early 1744 and in short order the two couples became friends.[6]

---

[5] Ibid.; *The A to Z of Georgian London* (London, England: London Topographical Society, 1982), 21; Old Bailey, see Note 4.
[6] Old Bailey, see Note 4.

Life was hard for the working poor in Georgian London, particularly chimney sweeps, who were poorly paid, worked in dangerous conditions, and whose face, hands, and clothing seemed to be perpetually coated with black soot. Moreover, the work was seasonal. By and large, chimneys were cleaned in the summer, when not in use. To make a living in winter, sweeps became ill-paid "nightmen" who had the unpleasant (and unhealthy) task of emptying privies or collecting the contents of chamber pots ("night soil") of households in an era when there was no indoor plumbing. Although these circumstances do not excuse what happened next, they certainly go a long way toward explaining why my ancestor and his friends turned to a life of crime.

In late March 1744, Haycraft and Smytheman decided that they would burglarize a shop owned by William and Ann Griffiths. If Smytheman's testimony can be trusted, it was not their first such "job." The location of the Griffiths' shop is uncertain but it was probably situated in Westminster where the robbers lived, or Holborn where they "fenced" the stolen goods. Smytheman later claimed that Ann Henley originally proposed the scheme whereas she said the robbery was his idea.[7] In either case, it seems clear that the motive was simply to obtain far more money than either Smytheman or Haycraft could earn legally by sweeping chimneys, selling soot, or cleaning privies.

---

[7] Ibid.

At about ten o'clock on the night of Thursday, April 5, 1744 (old style), Haycraft used a hammer to break the lock that secured the door of Griffiths' shop. Acting as lookouts, the two women waited outside in the street while their "husbands" took their time looting the shop. Apparently, no one disturbed them because it was not until after midnight that the two men finally emerged, carrying either a trunk or a sack full of penknives, metal buckles, cheap jewelry, and a variety of similar items, which they initially took to Smytheman's and Eaton's residence on Petty France.[8]

At four o'clock on the morning of April 6, Ann Griffiths was "called up" to find "my shop broke open." Later that day, she somehow learned that Haycraft and Smytheman had given away some of the stolen goods. This prompted the Griffiths to obtain a search warrant from a Justice Poulson,[9] who either resided or presided at Kirby Street, near Hatton Garden.

That same day, apparently, the youthful thieves went to Holborn, "overagainst Gray's-Inn Gate," where they first tried to sell the stolen goods to a stallholder for 20 shillings. Rejecting an offer of only 8 shillings, Eaton and Henley next approached a shopkeeper named Francis Whiting, telling him they had some hardware to sell. He agreed to meet them later in a nearby alehouse. When Whiting arrived, Haycraft and Smytheman were there as well. Probably over drinks,

---

[8] Ibid.
[9] Ibid.

he agreed to give them 17 shillings, 6 pence for the stolen items, which was accepted and promptly divided, "share and share alike." At the same meeting Whiting asked if they had any "wipes," meaning handkerchiefs. "If they had," Eaton later testified, they were to come back to the alehouse on Wednesday and Whiting would "buy them of them, and give them as much as any body would."[10]

Armed with a search warrant, a parish constable named Thomas Rawlins discovered the stolen goods in Whiting's shop window in Holborn. After Ann Griffiths identified the items stolen from her shop, Whiting and the four robbers were apprehended and taken to Newgate Prison,[11] located on the site of today's Central Criminal Court Building, which is popularly known as the "Old Bailey." Ironically, the place of their incarceration was only a short distance from the scene of their crime.

Of the British capital's fourteen prisons, Newgate— "Massive, dark and solemn—was "the most ancient and notorious." From all accounts, its reputation as "hell upon earth,"[12] was more than well-deserved. Male prisoners were kept in one of three holds. Which one depended upon whether or not a prisoner could pay the "Customary Dues of the Gaol." There were two holds for women. In all the

---

[10] Ibid.

[11] Ibid.

[12] Hepworth Dixon, *The London Prisons* (London, England: Jackson & Walford, 1850), 192; Thomas Elwood, *The History of the Life of Thomas Elwood* (London, England: W. & F. G. Cash, 1855), 142.

holds, "stinking, dark and dismal," the unfortunate prisoners, largely members of the lower class driven to lives of crime by their poverty, slept on the stone or oak planked floors. Those awaiting transportation, "knowing their time to be short here, rather than bestow one Minute toward cleaning [the ward], suffer themselves to live far worse than swine…for they are always poisoned with their own filth."[13]

Newgate prison drawing; courtesy British Library, London, England.

Those awaiting trial had "heavy iron manacles…clapped on their hands and feet" and were thrust into the "hold," a dark room with a stone floor, which "was entered by a hatch measuring fifteen by twenty feet." Inside was a single, long "barrack bed" on which a prisoner could sleep if they could stand the smell. Disorderly prisoners were chained to ring bolts placed around the room, from which they would be released provided they were willing and able to pay a fee to the jailor or "turnkey." Removal of the manacles also required payment of a fee.[14]

---

[13] B. L. of Twickenham, *An Accurate Description of Newgate* (London, England: t. Warner, 1724), 42-5.
[14] Coldham, Emigrants in Chains, 20.

18th century courtroom scene at the Old Bailey, London; from Arthur Haywood, *Lives of the Most Remarkable Criminals* (1735).

Fortunately for the four young burglars, justice was reasonably swift. On April 12, 1744, Justice Poulson questioned them. Each one confessed his or her role in the crime, although at first Haycraft claimed that he and Smytheman had found the items in a trunk while on their way home from an early morning sweeping job.[15]

At their subsequent trial, held on May 10, 1744, William and Ann Griffiths, Thomas Rawlins, and Francis Whiting testified against them. Although some of their own statements were contradictory, there seems no doubt that all four young people were guilty as charged and not surprisingly, Haycraft and Smytheman were so found, as was Eaton. Whiting was bound over for trial at the next session, "for receiving those goods knowing them to be stolen."[16]

Surprisingly, Ann Henley was acquitted. However, she was not immediately released but "kept in custody to be evidence against" Whiting at his trial on July 28. Remarkably, he was also acquitted, after several character witnesses attested to his honesty.[17] What became of Henley afterwards is uncertain but it is interesting to note that on January 18, 1746, a woman by that name was released from the House of Corrections at Clerkenwell after paying a one

---

[15] Old Bailey, see Note 4.

[16] Old Bailey Proceedings Online (www.oldbaileyonline.org, Version 6.0, 10 March 2012), July 1744, trial of Francis Whiting (t17440728-30).

[17] Ibid.

shilling fee.[18] There seems to be no evidence she ever left England and joined her "husband" in America.

As punishment for their crime, Haycraft, Smytheman, and Eaton, along with twenty other petty criminals, were sentenced to seven years "transportation" to America. They were fortunate. Five people who stood trial at the same court session were sentenced to death, no doubt by hanging. One was sentenced to fourteen years transportation. Another was ordered to be branded or "burnt in the hand."[19]

> SATURDAY 19. S.W.
> At the Old Bailey Seffions, received Sentence of Death, *Henry Cole*, for returning from Tranfportation (*Hugh Connor*, capitally convicted for a private Robbery, was refpited, as fome Doubt arofe about the Burglary) *Sarah Lowther*, for counterfeiting a Seaman's Will: *Ann Terry*, for murdering her Female Child; *Robert Rocket* for Street Robberies, and *Robert Fuller*, for fhouting a Man: 16 were caft for Tranfportation, 20 acquitted, and 1 burnt in the Hand.

This notice, which appeared in the *Gentleman's Magazine* for May 1744, records the outcome of the trials at which James Haycraft and others were sentenced to transportation. The number was actually 22, not 16 as shown.

---

[18] London Lives, 1690 to 1800: Crime, poverty and Social Policy in the Metropolis; Middlesex Sessions: Sessions papers—Justices' Working Documents, SM/PS, January 17 46, LL ref: LMSMPS503670O02 [http://www.londonlives.org/browse jsp?div=LMSMps 503 67ps503 670002; accessed 01 April 2015].

[19] Old Bailey, see Note 4.

In *An Accurate Description of Newgate* (1724), "B. L. of Twickenham" explained how the various sentences were arrived at:

> The limited time for Transportation is generally in proportion to the Offence, viz, if for Felony, Seven years; and for those who are under Sentence of Death, or such who buy Stole [sic] Goods, (knowing the same to be Stoln [sic] Fourteen years; and for such Criminals whose Actions appear to be very enormously Wicked, and are repreived [sic] after Condemnation, they are generally Transported for Term of Life.[20]

Although criminals had been "transported" to America as early as the mid-seventeenth century, it was not until after Parliament passed the 1718 Transportation Act (a.k.a., the statute of 4th of George I") that "persons convicted of burglary, robbery, perjury, forgery, and theft" were routinely "transported to the American plantations, for seven, or fourteen years, or for life." Not everyone approved of this practice. Throughout America, the exposure of their lives and property to all the convicted villains in England excited the indignation of the colonists. However, despite the "severe animadversions" that the Americans may have expressed in regard to transportation, British lawmakers held that the system not only enabled Britain to get rid of its surplus lawbreakers but also benefited the colonies, where

---

[20] B. L. of Twickenham, 49-50.

common laborers were in short supply. Moreover, by providing them with a new career, a new country, and a chance of reformation, the convicts would likewise benefit. Altogether, an "estimated …50,000 convicts came over on ships owned by hired contractors.[21] Here is how it was done:

> The Commencing of the Time of Transportation, is accounted from the Day the Keeper of Newgate delivers the criminals out of his Gaol, to the Captain who transports them to the places assigned.
> At the Captain's receiving them out of Newgate, they (being Hand-cuff'd two and two together) are directed to the Transport Ship; between the Decks of which is a prison or Gaol, wherein they are strongly secured, till such time as they arrive at the intended port, being allow'd each Day such Subsistance [sic] as is requisite for them.[22]

Sometime in May 1744, probably either at Rotherhithe or Deptford, Haycraft was taken in chains aboard the *Justitia*, a 260-ton British prison hulk. Altogether, twenty-five people were sentenced to transportation in Middlesex County Court between February and May. It is probable that all were transported aboard the *Justitia*.[23]

---

[21] Timothy Pitkin, *A Political and Civil History of the United States of America, Vol. 1* (New Haven, Connecticut: Hezekiah Howe and Durrie & Peck, 1828), 133-4; Justin McCarthy, *A History of Our Own Times* (New York: Harper and Brothers, 1850), 22; Forty-ninth Congress, Second Session, *Report of the Secretary of the Interior, Vol. V* (Washington, D.C.: Government Printing Office, 1887),474; Frederick Converse Beach, ed., *The Encyclopedia Americana* (New York: Scientific American Compiling Dept., 1904-05), "30. United States-Slavery In."

[22] B. L. of Twickenham, 50.

[23] Peter Wilson Coldham, Bonded passengers to America, vol. II, Middlesex, 1 6 1 7- 1 775 (Baltimore, Maryland: Genealogical Publishing Company, 1983), 7, 14, 27, 39, 45, 51, 60, 61, 86, 96, 99,106, 113,

Transported convicts being readied to go aboard ship in London; from *The New & Complete Newgate Calendar* (1795).

As the *Justitia,* one of two convict fleet "flagships" (the other was the *Tryal*),[24] sailed down the River Thames toward the sea, it seems unlikely that James Haycraft and his fellow transportees, no doubt chained together in a dark, dank hold below decks, were able to take a last look at their English homeland. I cannot help but wonder what James was thinking as the voyage began. Did he think he might return to London some day? (He didn't.) Was Ann Henley, the "wife" the hapless young chimney sweep was forced to

---

126 (James Haycraft listed this page), 140, 147, 169, 203, 210, 229, 249, 252 & 329.
[24] Peter Wilson Coldham, *Emigrants in Chains*, (Baltimore, Maryland: Genealogical Publishing Company, 1992), 104.

leave behind, in his thoughts? Surely, she must have been. And did Ann likewise think of James as she sat in a Newgate Prison cell, knowing that the last time they would probably ever see one another was in the courtroom? Unfortunately, we are left only to imagine.

18th century British ship taking on passengers; courtesy Library of Congress.

Although the situation in which he found himself was unfortunate to say the least, James Haycraft probably did not know that it could have been far worse. On April 17, 1744, only five days after James and his friends were sentenced, the previous captain of the *Justitia*, Barent Bond, was himself brought to trial on four counts of "murder on the high seas." The charge stemmed from a voyage a little more than a year earlier, when 163 convicted felons and indentured servants were brought aboard. The ill treatment they received at the hands of Bond during the voyage to America resulted in no less than forty-five deaths. Remarkably, despite a preponderance of evidence against him, the sadistic captain was acquitted, but he "never again" worked "in the transportation trade, at least in England." Afterward, Bond went to America, where he acquired some property in Maryland before returning to London, where he died in 1749.[25]

Jack Campbell, about whom nothing is known, was Bond's replacement as captain of the *Justitia* when the vessel crossed the Atlantic in the spring of 1744.[26] Whether he treated his unwilling passengers any better or any worse than his predecessor, I am unable to say. In either event, we know that James Haycraft and Samuel Smytheman survived the voyage, which lasted from six to eight weeks, because they both have descendants living in the United States today. (What became of Elizabeth Eaton is unknown.) Although official records only name "America" as its destination, at the end of the voyage the *Justitia* probably anchored at Leeds Town, on the Rappahannock River.[27]

---

[25] Ibid., 108-10; *Maryland Historical Magazine, Vol. IV* (Baltimore, Maryland: The Maryland Historical Society, 1909), 196.

[26] Coldham, *Emigrants in Chains*, 174.

[27] Although there are apparently no extant copies of the *Virginia Gazette* for 1744, some later editions contain notices advertising the sale of indentured servants just arrived at Leeds Town aboard the

Upon arrival, Campbell set about ridding himself of his unfortunate passengers, "selling" them at auction to the highest bidder, undoubtedly to be used in most cases as laborers on tobacco plantations until the expiration of the term of their sentence. The way this was accomplished was described in a book about Newgate Prison:

> At their coming into the Bay, the Captain sends his Boat ashore, to this Factor or Correspondent, who comes on Board, to whom the Captain delivers the List he received at Newgate, of the several Persons delivered to him, and upon View of the same, an Examination is made of what Number (if any) died in their Passage, what are remaining Alive, and in what Condition they are; which Inspection being made (and a Receipt or Discharge being given from the Merchant or Factor to the Captain for the same) Notice is immediately given to all the Planters, and other Inhabitants...who thereupon come on Board and take a View of every Person to be disposed of, and after having chosen such as they think for their Purpose, an Agreement is made for them, and the Money paid, which for each person, is from 20 s. to 10 l. The Price always in proportion to the Health, Age, and Trade of the Person.[28]

And here is an additional description of the process:

> They are placed together in a Row, like so many oxen or cows, and the Planters come and survey them; and if they like 'em, they agree for price with the person entrusted with the selling of 'em. And after they have paid the money, they ask

---

Justitia. See the *Virginia Gazette* for November 12, 1767, March 28, 1771, and March 18, 1775.

[28] *An Accurate Description of Newgate* (London, England: Printed for T. Warner at the Black Boy in Pater Noster Row, 1724), 51.

'em if they like him for Master and is willing to go with him. If they answer in the Affirmative, they are delivered to him as his Property. If, on the contrary, as sometimes happens, they should answer in the Negative, the Planter has his money again and another Planter may make choice of him, whom he may likewise refuse, but no more, for with the Third it seems, he is obliged to go, whether he likes him or not. As there are frequently People who run away from their Masters, there is a reward of twenty shillings paid for the taking of 'em, which makes it very difficult for 'em to escape. When a Master gives them a discharge, he always gives them a Pass, by the Authority of which they may safely go anywhere; and without one, they are liable to be put into a Gaol and confin'd for some days to see if any Enquiry be made after them.[29]

One felon, sentenced in 1738, later described the process in a book he wrote about his experiences:

The Captain ordered a Gun to be fired as a Signal for the Planters to come down, and then went ashore; he soon after sent on board a Hogshead of Rum and order'd all the Men Convicts to be close shaved against the next Morning, and the Women to have their best Head Dresses put on, which occasion'd no little Hurry on board, for between the Trimming of Beards and the putting on of Caps, all hands were fully employed. In the morning the Captain ordered publick Notice to be given of a Day of Sale; the Convicts, who were pretty near a Hundred, were all ordered upon Deck, where a large Bowl of Punch was made, and the Planters flock'd on board.[30]

---

[29] The Ordinary of Newgate, *His Account of the Behaviour, Confession, and Dying Words, of the Malefactors Who were Executed at Tyburn, on Wednesday the 7th of November, 1744, Being the Fourth Execution in the Mayoralty of the Right Honble. Sir Robert Westley, Knt., Lord Mayor of the City of London, Number IV. For the said Year.* (London: Printed and Sold by John Applebee, in Bolt-Court, near the Leg-Tavern, Fleet-street. 1744.), 5.

[30] Robert Goady, *The Surprising Adventures of Bampfylde Moore Carew, King of the Beggars* (London,

Cultivation of tobacco in colonial Virginia: from David B. Scott, *A School History of the United States, from the Discovery of America to the Year 1878.*

Some researchers believe that James Haycraft was indentured first to George Neville, a planter who in 1743 obtained 181 acres of land "beginning on the west side of the Bull Run Mountain on the drains of Broad Run" in Prince William County. "Neville's Ordinary," a colonial inn reportedly owned by Neville and visited on at least one occasion by George Washington (during the time he worked as a surveyor), is clearly shown on a 1751 map of Virginia drawn by Joshua Fry and Peter Jefferson (*not* Thomas Jefferson as some sources mistakenly report) and printed by

---

England: W. Salter, 1817), 84.

Thomas Jeffreys, "Geographer to his Royal Highness the Prince of Wales."[31]

In 1759 George Neville's land became part of newly formed Fauquier County. Later, some say, Haycraft's "master" reportedly became George's son, John, who after reaching adulthood and getting married, moved west to neighboring Frederick County, where he served as sheriff.[32]

As it happens, there is no evidence that James Haycraft was ever indentured to either George or John Neville. The alleged connection is entirely conjecture, based on the fact of John Neville's becoming guardian of the Haycraft children following their parents' deaths. That George Neville was supposedly Haycraft's first master appears to be deduced from the fact that John Neville was only thirteen-years-old (born July 26, 1731) when James Haycraft arrived in America in 1744, which means that he could not have been the one to who James was originally indentured.[33]

All this being said, evidence has recently come to light that confirms the name of the man to whom James Haycraft *was* indentured, and he *wasn't* a Neville. This evidence is in

---

[31] 1751 Map of Virginia, drawn by Joshua Fry and Peter Jefferson, and printed by Thomas Jeffreys, "Geographer to His Royal Highness, the Prince of Wales," map collection, Library of Congress, Washington, D.C.

[32] Edward Purcell, *Who Was Who in the American Revolution* (New York, New York: Facts on File, Inc., 1993), 348.

[33] Haycraft, Jr., 120-1.

the form of two entries in Frederick County, Virginia court records.

The first, dated May 14, 1751, is a court order that reads: "On the complaint of James Haycraft ag't. Thomas Waters his master, for misusing him. It is ordered that unless the sd. Thomas Waters cloath his sd. servant better and give him better usage, that on the next just complaint, he be ordered to be sold."[34]

The second entry, dated June 4, 1752, records a complaint by Haycraft against Waters that was dismissed on account of neither party appearing in court on the appointed day.[35] This suggests that whatever the nature of the second complaint, Haycraft's master addressed it to his satisfaction without the need to involve the county court. The more likely reason, however, is that by the time the court was prepared to hear the complaint, Haycraft's term of service had expired and therefore, he was no longer Waters' servant.

It also appears that James Haycraft was married sometime shortly after his indenture expired in 1751, at which time he was about thirty-two years of age. Together, he and his wife, whose name has been lost to history, had four children—one daughter that died in infancy and three sons: James, Samuel, and Joshua. Our only other evidence of James Haycraft's presence in Frederick County is the will

---
[34] Frederick County, Virginia, Court Order Book 3, p.428.
[35] Frederick County, Virginia, Court Order Book 4, p.159.

of a man named James Taylor, which Haycraft witnessed on 18 October 1760.[36] After James and his wife died about 1762, John Neville took the three boys into his household and cared for them until they reached their majority.[37]

Some researchers (including me) have wondered if the reason that John Neville became the Haycraft brothers' guardian was not because he was James Haycraft's master (which we now know he wasn't) but rather, because he was the boys' uncle by marriage. In short, it has been speculated that James Haycraft's wife was none other than John Neville's sister. Unfortunately, there is little likelihood of that being the case owing to the fact that John Neville had six brothers and only one sister, Ann, who reportedly married a fellow named William O'Bannon.[38]

Whatever John Neville's reasons might have been for taking the Haycraft brothers into his home, the three boys almost certainly could not have been more fortunate. From all accounts, Neville was an educated man "of very frank and hearty address, of sound judgement, of much firmness and decision of character" as well as "of plain, blunt manners, [and] a pleasant companion." It was said too that he was a great storyteller, able to "give interest" even "to trifling incidents." Several biographers have called attention

---

[36] J. Estelle Stewart, *Abstracts of Wills, Inventories, and Administration Accounts of Frederick County, Virginia, 1743-1800* (Baltimore: Genealogical Publishing Company, 1980), 128.
[37] Haycraft, Jr., 121.
[38] Genealogy Research Papers prepared by William G. Scroggins, John Neville <http://wgscroggins.kueber.us/Neville1_John_born_1662.pdf>[Accessed 03 March 2012.]

to his "early acquaintance of Washington, both of whom were about the same age," which apparently led him to join the future president in General Braddock's ill-fated expedition against the French in 1755. John Neville's son Presley, with whom the Haycraft brothers grew up, is reported to have also been an "accomplished gentleman."[39]

---

[39] Neville B. Craig, *The History of Pittsburgh* (Pittsburgh, Pennsylvania: John H. Mellor, Bookseller & Stationer, 1851), 124 & 230.

The Malevolent Magistrate

Although most of my ancestors that came to America from Europe were English, Irish, Scottish or Welsh—in other words, British—some, as pointed out in the chapter entitled "Captive in the Catskills," were Dutch or French. Another, as I revealed in the chapter entitled "The Runaway Servant," was German. As it happens, he was but one of three German forebears that I know of.

One of the other two was a young man named Konradt Wiedt, who at the age of twenty-five, sometime in the late summer of 1743, embarked along with 199 other so-called "Palatinates" aboard a ship called the *Lydia*, James Abercrombie, Master, at the Dutch port of Rotterdam. Following a brief stop at the English port of Cowes, on the Isle of Wight, the ship arrived at Philadelphia (which was then the largest city in all of the British colonies in America) on Friday, September 20.[1] Shortly after arrival, Konrad, along with all the other passengers aboard the *Lydia*, swore an oath of allegiance, as required by law, to His Majesty, King George II of Great Britain and Ireland. Sometime later, my newly-arrived 7th Great-Grandfather Anglicized his name to "Conrad Wheat."

---

[1] *The Pennsylvania Gazette* and *The Pennsylvania Journal*, September 22, 1743.

The Palatinate or *Pfalz*, from which my ancestor originated, was and still is a province or state in the southwestern corner of present-day Germany. It is popularly known as the "Rhineland," owing to the fact that the Rhine River forms the boundary between the Palatinate and France. In 1743, the Palatinate was an independent principality. At that time, there was no nation of Germany as we know it today. Back then, present-day Germany was a patchwork quilt of individual principalities and small kingdoms. It was not unified until 1871.

Apparently, Conrad Wheat arrived in America as an indentured servant (or became one shortly after arrival), just like Peter Dantzer—and when I say "just like Peter Dantzer," I mean that *Conrad also ran away*! In mid-July 1744, less than a year after he came ashore at Philadelphia, his master, George Kastner, who lived at Germantown in Philadelphia County, placed an advertisement in a German language newspaper—*Der Hoch-Deutsche Pensylvanische Geschicht-Schreiber*—in which he offered a reward of two Pounds for the return of his servant, describing Conrad as about thirty years old, medium stature, and with brown hair.[2] Did anyone collect the reward? Or did Conrad somehow manage to avoid capture? Unfortunately, I don't know. Nor do I know where he spent most of the next twenty years. All I can say for certain is that somewhere

---

[2] *Der Hoch-Deutsche Pensylvanische Geschicht-Schreiber*, Germantown, Pennsylvania, July 16, 1744.

along the way he got married and started a family that included a daughter named Catherine. This is her story, and Conrad's too, and indeed the entire Conrad Wheat family's.

****

At some point in his life, Conrad Wheat and his family moved to Frederick County, Maryland, which is fifty miles northwest of Baltimore and immediately adjacent to Adams County, Pennsylvania. This was during the same time that surveyors Charles Mason and Jeremiah Dixon were busy establishing, once and for all, the official boundary between Pennsylvania and Maryland, popularly known as the "Mason-Dixon" line. After the northern states, including Pennsylvania, abolished slavery, this boundary also became the dividing line between free and slave states, which collectively took the title "Dixie Land," or simply "Dixie." It is generally held that Dixon's name was the origin of this regional appellation.

In any event, it was in Frederick County, Maryland, on July 9, 1762, that Conrad Wheat entered into a four-year agreement to rent a piece of property called "Matson's Devise" at a rate of 50 shillings per year. His landlord was Capt. Evan Shelby, a Welsh-born fur trapper, frontiersman, and one of several Frederick County magistrates. Shelby's military title dated from the French and Indian War, when he served as a scout on the ill-fated Braddock expedition into what is now Western Pennsylvania. In 1762, Wheat's family consisted of his wife, Margaret, and at least five children, one of which was a daughter, Catherine, who is one of the central figures in this story.

HARVESTING WITH THE SICKLE IN COLONIAL DAYS
A colonial farm family, at work in their field; from Frank P. Bachman, *Great Inventors and Their Inventions* (New York: American Book Co., 1918).

Precisely how old Catherine Wheat was when the following described episode took place is unknown, but it is obvious that she was at least old enough to become pregnant and give birth, which is what started the whole business.

At the September 1764 term of the Frederick County court, held in the town of Frederick, Catherine Wheat "charged Thomas Hynes, on Oath, before Capt. Thomas Price, one of his Lordship's Justices of this County, with being the Father of her Bastard Child." Upon hearing the accusation, Price ordered both Catherine and the alleged father to appear in court at the November term, but when Hynes showed up and Catherine didn't, the matter was deferred until March 1765. "In the interim," young Hynes went to see Evan Shelby, and asked him in his capacity as magistrate to issue a warrant that would allow him (Hynes) to take the child from Catherine.

When Hynes asked for Shelby's help, he (Shelby) summarily issued a "Search Warrant for Stolen Goods." So, then what happened?

According to four eyewitnesses—John Barkley, Peter Steed, George Rush, and Henry Rush—it was on Monday evening, December 2, 1764, that Constable Barnett Johnson and five other men—Edmund Moran, James Dawson, Nathan Lynn, John Gerloh and Thomas Hynes, the alleged father of the child—went to Conrad Wheat's house, "between the Hours of Nine and Ten o'Clock at Night, and asked for a Quart of Whiskey, and got but a Pint." Whereupon, according to the "evidences" (as witnesses were termed in those days), the six:

…then asked if there was a Pedlar there, then they called Conrod Wheat out a Doors, and asked him if he would [give] up his Daughter's Child. He asked them upon what Condition, they answered they had an Order from the Court for the Child, Conrod Wheat demanded to see the Order, then Edmund Moran read the Order then Conrod Wheat found the Order was from Evan Shelby Esqr and not from the Court, and refused to let the Child go, as the Girl had given Security to the Court which he thought was Sufficient, then the Constable Commanded to lay hold, then some began to Stop the People belonging to the House from endeavouring to save the Child then they began to Riot and Beat the People of the House, and Thomas Hynes Swore he would have the Child Dead or alive then they hurt one of the Children belonging to the House then One of his Girls took his own Child and ran out of the Store Room into the Kitchen and the Rioters all followed her and the People of the House Shut the Door after them, and forewarned them from Coming in again, then they broke open the Door and Came in by Force, and then they began to beat the People of the House till some of them was not able to go to the Justice, and Thomas Hynes beat Margaret Wheat, the Mother of the Child and Swore he would be the Death of her. And then Nathan Lynn took the Child and ran out of the Doors with it, and then one of the Women belonging to the House got the Child and ran out into the field and Barnett Johnson and John Gerloh, ran after her and beat her, and took the Child from her, and then they came to the House of Ralph Matson where Evan Shelby was, and the Constable took the Child and delivered to Capt Evan Shelby, and he delivered it to William Hynes, and Thomas Hynes, was heard say that he made the Dutch Bitches Blood flye and Christian Matson asked Evan Shelby if the Girl had not a Right to keep the Child if she Could get Security to keep the Child off the Parish, and Evan Shelby made answer that she Could get no Security, and refused Joseph Flint, and Thomas Brooks, likewise Evan Shelby said if he ever Catched Conrod Wheat in Maryland he would have him Cropped for disobeying his

Orders, and not delivering up the Child and said if he had gone he would have burnt his House over his Head likewise William Hynes, and Thomas Hynes gave Evan Shelby a Bond of One hundred Pounds in behalf of his Lord-ship to keep the Child off the Parish.

P.S. When they came before Joseph Warford, in order to have their Trial Evan Shelby demanded a Warrant of Joseph Warford for the Girl's fine but Joseph Warford refused to grant it, then Evan Shelby Writ one himself and Demanded Joseph Warford to sign it, but, he refused Then Evan Shelby sign'd it and she was Taken and Thomas Hynes gave his Note to Evan Shelby for her fine. [3]

Following the invasion of his home, the kidnapping of his grandchild, and the beating of himself and other members of his family, Conrad Wheat complained to Magistrate Joseph Warford. What happened next is almost comical:

That upon Complaint of Conrad Wheate and the others who had been beaten Hynes and the other Rioters were brought before Mr Joseph Warford, where finding the matter more serious than they had imagined, and likely to become a Court Business, Thomas Hynes gets the Girl on his Lap, and (as Mr Warford writes in his narrative) was very Sweet. Whereupon Mr Warford Advised the young Man, to a Marriage, which was at Length agreed upon, the Girl's Father promising to give the young Couple £30 & a £5 Wedding.

That during these Transactions, Capt Shelby demanded of Joseph Warford a Warrant for the young Woman's fine, which Mr Warford refused to Grant he also refused to sign one drawn

---

[3] William Hand Browne, ed., *Archives of Maryland, Volume 32, Proceedings of the Council of Maryland April 5, 1761 - September 16, 1770* (Baltimore, Maryland: Maryland Historical Society, 1913), 155-6.

up by Capt Shelby, and presented to him for that purpose. Whereupon the Capt Signed it himself, had her immediately taken into Custody, and again discharged her on receiving a Promissory note from Thomas Hynes for the amount of her fine.

That Cap' Shelby at Length proceeded to the Marriage Ceremony, which he performed by asking the young Man whether he would take that Woman to his lawful Wedded Wife? and put the same Question, mutatis mutandis to the young Woman; after which he pronounced them to be lawful Man & Wife, saying Jump Dog, Leap Bitch, and I'll be damned if all the Men on Earth can unmarry you. That the new married Couple were put to bed in Mr Warford's own Bed, with the usual Ceremonies of throwing the Stocking &c. Mrs. Warford having previously received five Shillings for the use of the said Bed. And the whole Proceedings on the Riot &c. quashed at once.

That some time after the young Couple had been left to themselves, the young Man wanted to leave his Consort: and opening the Door would have come out. But was prevented by Capt Shelby, who opposed him with a fork in his hand, which he threatened to jobb into his Cutts if he attempted to leave his Wife. Whereupon the young fellow retired peaceably, and was found by the Company early in the Morning fast asleep in Bed with his Consort.[4]

Six other witnesses—Joshua Meaks, Archibald Flegor, William Hart, Christian Matson, John Pac, and Elizabeth Warford—attested to the above-described, saying:

> There was a sort of a Riot Committed by Thomas Hynes and others against Conrod Wheat, his Family much abused they was taken by a precept and brought before me and was like to be bound over to Court, but to Serene themselves Thomas Hynes gets the Girl on his Lap and was very Sweet, I seeing that

---
[4] Ibid., 133-4.

says to Hynes as you have Spoiled this Girl and taken her Credit from her you ought to Marry her, he said I have not much against it I will Consider of it, the Father of the Girl made answer that he would give them thirty Pounds and a five Pound Weding, and upon the whole they agreed to be Married as the Evidences tells me they was fairly Married by Evan Shelby Esq[rs][5]

Despite this apparent though crude resolution of the matter at hand, six of Evan Shelby's fellow Frederick County magistrates—Andrew Hugh, William Blair, Peter Bainbridge, T. Dickson, Thomas Price, and William Luckett—soon after sent a petition to the Governor of Maryland, Horatio Sharpe, giving a brief description of the incident and complaining of "a Scandalous Abuse of…Power" on the part of Captain Shelby, as well as Joseph Warford, asking:

> That a review of the above recited Transaction may be sufficient to shew how incapable either of the above mentioned Persons are to sustain the dignified Character wherewith they are invested; and how unworthy of that high Trust which their ignorance of the Laws, whereby the Community is to be regulated, their assuming to themselves Powers with which they are not invested, and their turning the Execution of their Office by indirect Means to their own private Emolument and the scandal of Public Justice, have so grossly abused.
> Your Petitioners therefore humbly pray that the aforesaid Captain Evan Shelby, and Mr. Joseph Warford may be left out of the Commission for the Peace in Frederick County, that the

---

[5] Ibid., 156-7.

whole Body (otherwise, We hope, respectable) may not be wounded thro' their Sides or laughed at as their Associates.[6]

Shortly after receiving this petition, the Governor directed his clerk, Upton Scott, to compose and send the following response to the six magistrates:

> Gentlemen
> I am Ordered by the Governor and Council to inform you, that in Considering a Petition preferred to his Excellency by you, complaining of the Behaviour of Capt Evan Shelby and Mr Joseph Warford two Magistrates of Frederick County, they observe the following Words made use of Viz^t "without insisting upon other Irregularties" which contain an Insinuation that there are other matters of Complaint against these Gentlemen, besides those set forth in your Petition, and as they propose to make a full enquiry into the Truth of the Misbehaviour of these Magistrates, they desire that you will transmit to them whatever further Charges you have against the said Capt Shelby and Mr Warford, in Order that the whole may be examined together.[7]

At the same time, apparently, Governor Sharpe also ordered his clerk to inform Shelby and Warford "of the Complaint made against them, and to Deliver them Copies of the Different Papers Containing the Accusations against them if they desire it," adding that if "these Gentlemen Chuse to Enter into a Justification of their Conduct, the third

---

[6] Ibid., 132-3.
[7] Ibid., 133-4.

Thursday in October next is fixed upon to hear the Parties of which they are to have timely Notice."[8]

On August 11, 1766, after Shelby apparently denied the charges, Governor Sharpe Governor ordered the clerk to "Write the following Letter to John Darnall Esqr Clerk of Frederick County."[9]

> Sir
>   I am directed by the Governor and Council to Acquaint the Magistrates of your County who lately preferred a Complaint against Cap Evan Shelby and Mr Joseph Warford two Members of their Body that Mr Shelby having denied the Truth of several of the Facts alledged against him, they will on Thursday the 16th of October next examine into the Foundation of the Complaint, you will be pleased to Communicate this to these Gentlemen at the next Meeting of your Court, that if they chuse to support the Accusation they may take proper Measures for that purpose.[10]

Although as noted above, a hearing was originally scheduled to be held on October 16, 1766 in the Colonial Council chamber in Annapolis, for reasons that seem to have been lost to history, it was postponed until November 1st. Here is an official transcript of the proceedings, at which apparently only one of the accused magistrates, Joseph Warford, actually appeared in person:

---

[8] Ibid., 157.
[9] Ibid., 133-4.
[10] Ibid.

At a Council held at the Council Chamber on Saturday the 1st day of November in the sixteenth year of his Lordship's Dominion Anno Domini 1766.

Present
His Excellency Horatio Sharpe Esqr Governor.
The honble Benjamin Tasker, Daniel Dulany, John Ridout, Chas Goldsborough and Henry Hooper Esq^{rs}

Daniel Dulany Esqr and the Clerk of this Board take and Subscribe the Oath of Abjuration directed to be taken by the late Act of Parliament. Mr Joseph Warford being called in and Examined in Relation to the Complaint preferred against him by the Magistrates of Frederick County, This Board in Consideration of his being very illiterate and keeping an Ordinary* is of Opinion that he is not a Person properly Qualified to be a Magistrate and recommend to his Excellency that he be left out of the Commission.[11]

[*Author's note: An "ordinary" was a tavern or alehouse.]

The reason why Shelby did not also appear, is explained in an earlier petition, in which the accused man wrote:

To His Excellency Horatio Sharpe Esqr and the honourable the Members of his Lordships Council.

The Petition of Evan Shelby of Frederick County.

Sheweth.
That Whereas several Magistrates of Frederick County have laid a Complaint against your Petitioner before your Excellency

---

[11] Ibid., 166.

and Honours, which was to have been examined into at this time, your Petitioner humbly prays that a longer time may be given and that the Evidences according to the List annexed may be summoned to attend, for tho' your Petitioner will not presume to exculpate himself entirely from every private failing or Public Indiscretion they have accused him with yet he hopes to make it appear that they are not of so deep a dye as they have represented them.

List of Evidences:
Thomas Bowles
John Cary
Arthur Charlton
Robert Wood
Joshua Meek
Barnet Johnson
Thomas Haynes [sic] [12]

Perhaps it was due to the high regard that Marylanders had for Captain Shelby on account of his military exploits that the Governor and his Council agreed to yield to Shelby's request. In any event, the governor's clerk was directed to issue the following summons to "the Sheriffs of Frederick County":

You are hereby required to Summons Thomas Bowles, John Cary, Arthur Charlton, Robert Wood, Joshua Meek, Barnet Johnson and Thomas Haynes that all Excuses set apart they make their Personal Appearance before the Governor and Council at the City of Annapolis on Monday the Eighth day of December next to Testify the Truth of their Knowledge on

---

[12] Ibid., 166.

behalf of Capᵗ Evan Shelby in a matter in Question depending before them. Hereof fail not at your Peril.
Annapolis 31ˢᵗ October 1766.
Signed p order
Upton Scott Cl: Con.[1]

While it may be that some of the other witnesses on Shelby's list testified before the Governor and his Council on December 8, it was not until the next day—December 9, 1766—slightly more than two years after the "riot" at Conrad Wheat's house occurred, that Thomas Hynes, the purported father of Catherine Wheat's baby was called upon to give his account of the incident and also his subsequent marriage to Catherine:

> Thomas Hynes Deposeth and saith, that he was present, at Ralph Matson's House, when the Constable of Linton Hundred brought the Child of Catharine Wheate and gave it to Capᵗ Shelby who delivered it to William Hynes, who Joined in a recognizance with the Deponent Security in a £100 to keep the Child from being a burthen on the County, and that he did not hear Capᵗ Shelby make use of any threatning Expressions against Conrod Wheat, or say any thing about burning the said Wheat's House. That he never heard, that Thomas Brooks and Joseph Flint offered to become security on the part of Catharine Wheat, or that Capᵗ Shelby refused to accept them as such. He further saith that he never gave any Note nor paid or assumed to pay to Capᵗ Shelby any Money for Catharine Wheat's fine, nor does he believe that any Warrant was issued by the said Capᵗ Shelby against Catharine Wheat on that Account. He further saith that on the last Evening of the Old year 1765 at the

---

[1] Ibid., 166-7.

House of Mr Joseph Warford after drinking pretty freely in a Numerous Company, M" Warford proposed that Capt Shelby should Marry this Deponent to Catharine Wheate and the rest of the Company approving much of the proposal and having got them together Joined their Hands when Capt Shelby asked each of them separately whether they were satisfied, and on their Signifying their Willingness he declared them to be Man and Wife, but that he heard nothing of his making use of any such Expressions as "Jump Dog, Leap Bitch and I'll be damned if all the Men on Earth can un Marry you" that he knows nothing nor ever heard of M$^{rs.}$ Warford's having received five Shillings for the use of her bed that Night, and further this Deponent saith not.

Sworn to this 9th of Decr 1766

Thos Hynes, before me. U Scott Cl: Con.[2]

****

Unfortunately, it appears that the testimony of the other witnesses who were called to speak on Shelby's behalf was not preserved. Neither does there seem to be any record of the Governor and Council's decision to either retain or dismiss Captain Shelby from his post as a magistrate of Frederick County.

Whether or not Evan Shelby lost his magistrate's commission, there's one thing we can be sure of: He remained Conrad Wheat's landlord, and in October 1766, he (Shelby) went to court in Frederick County to collect what he claimed was four years back rent dating from July 9, 1762, a total of 10 Pounds, 12 shillings and 6 pence.

Did he get his money? Did Conrad pay up?

---

[2] Ibid., 173.

Again, I don't know. All that's seemingly been preserved (in the Library of Congress, no less!) is the demand.

However, there's one thing that I *am* sure of: Following the events described in this chapter, Conrad Wheat decided to move. (Who can blame him, with a landlord like Evan Shelby!) In March 1767, he received a grant of 300 acres of land in Air Township, Cumberland County, Pennsylvania, about sixty-five miles north of Frederick County, Maryland.

In time, he would move again, nearly 300 miles west to Ohio County, Virginia, and what happened to him and his family after they arrived is chronicled in the chapter entitled "The Last Battle of the Revolution."

McIntosh's "Stepping Stone"

In the 1992 movie "Last of the Mohicans," which stars Daniel Day-Lewis and Wes Studi, there is a scene where Studi's character, a Huron Indian named *Magua*, tells his adversary, British Colonel Edmund Munro (portrayed in the film by actor Maurice Roëves), just as he is about to kill him in battle (and afterward cut out his heart), that he plans to also kill the Colonel's two daughters—Alice and Cora—so as "to wipe your seed from the earth forever." Thus, Munro's final thought, as he takes his last breath, is not only will *he* die, but also, with the killing of his daughters, *his entire bloodline will vanish*! In other words, *Magua* is telling him that he will have no descendants to remember him. As it happens, however, only one of the Colonel's daughters—Alice (portrayed by Jodhi May)—dies afterward, by stepping off a cliff rather than give *Magua* the satisfaction of clubbing her to death. Cora (played by actress Madeline Stowe) survives.

So far as I know, none of my ancestors were specially singled out for annihilation by a bitter, revengeful native warrior. Nevertheless, the bloodline of one—a soldier in the Continental Army during the American Revolution—came very close to disappearing, not with an Indian brutally knifing him to death, but rather, as a result of starvation, in a time and at a place that history has largely forgotten.

Here then, is another tale of survival, another story of an ancestor who, if he had died as a result of his encounter with Native Americans (see chapter, "Captive in the Catskills"), would have left no descendants, including me obviously, to write about him more than two hundred years later.

****

My 5th Great-Grandfather, Samuel Haycraft, Sr., born on November 19, 1752[1] in the British Colony of Virginia, was the middle son of James Haycraft, Jr., a London chimney sweep "transported" in 1744 to America, where upon arrival he was sold into seven years indentured servitude following his conviction in a London court on a charge of burglary. The name of Samuel's mother is unknown. The story of Samuel's father, James, is told, as you may recall, in an earlier chapter entitled "Transported!"

Samuel had three siblings: A sister named Catherine, who died in infancy, and two brothers: James Haycraft III (known in America as James Jr.), born in 1750; and Joshua,

---

[1] Haycraft Family Bible, Family Record "Births" page included as part of Margaret Van Meter Haycraft's application for a Revolutionary War pension based on her husband's service. In his celebrated book about the history of Elizabethtown, Kentucky, Samuel Jr. erroneously reported that his father was born on September 11. See Samuel Haycraft, Jr.'s *A History of Elizabethtown' Kentucky and Its Surroundings* (Elizabethtown, Kentucky: The Woman's Club of Elizabethtown, Kentucky, 1921), 121.

born in 1754. Their childhood home was Frederick County, Virginia, where their father is known to have resided.[2]

Samuel's mother and father died around 1762, when he was nine or ten years old. "Consequently," his son Samuel Jr. later wrote, "the children learned nothing about their ancestors beyond the vague impressions formed in infancy." The parents' place of burial has likewise been lost to history. For reasons that can only be guessed, John Neville, a wealthy Virginia planter, took the boys into his care and according to all accounts, "Samuel Haycraft [and presumably also his brothers] received a good common school education, and remained with Col. Nevill [sic] until he was of age, when, with a letter of recommendation, he started out to shift for himself in the world."[3]

In 1773, when Samuel Haycraft reached his majority, Frederick County, which is located in northwestern Virginia, was situated on the edge of what was then a raw frontier. This area—the Shenandoah River Valley—lies in the heart of what is even today one of the most scenic landscapes in North America. On the north it is bounded by the Potomac River, on the east by the lush, forest-covered Blue Ridge Mountains, and on the west by the North Ridge Mountains, also called the "Devil's Backbone." From the early eighteenth century up to the start of the Revolution in

---

[2] Ibid.

[3] J. M. Armstrong, *The Biographical Encyclopædia of Kentucky of the Dead and Living Men of the Nineteenth Century, Volume 1* (Cincinnati, Ohio: J. M Armstrong & Company, 1878), 222.

1775, hundreds of thousands of immigrants from England, Scotland, Wales, Ireland, and Germany passed through Frederick County and the Shenandoah River Valley, following the Great Wagon Road, which linked Philadelphia with the colonial "backcountry" of Pennsylvania, Virginia, North and South Carolina, and Northern Georgia. Today, the road is Interstate Highway 81. When these travelers reached Frederick County, some liked what they saw and stayed. Others moved on.

Lord Fairfax, an English aristocrat who owned thousands of acres of land in Northern Virginia and was the only English peer to make his home in America apparently liked Frederick County very much. In 1752, the very year in which Samuel Haycraft was born, Lord Fairfax went to live on a country estate called Greenway Court in Frederick County, where he remained for the rest of his very long life. (He died in 1781 at the age of eighty-eight.) Another well-known gentleman with close ties to Frederick County was future president George Washington, who first visited the Shenandoah Valley in 1748, while on a surveying expedition for Lord Fairfax. Washington ended up staying until 1765. During the very same time that Samuel Haycraft was growing up in that area, Washington maintained a surveying office in Winchester, the seat of Frederick County, and in 1758 and 1761, he was elected to represent the people of that district in Virginia's colonial legislature-the House of Burgesses. One of those people, of course, was Samuel Haycraft.

When Samuel Haycraft was not yet three years old, Robert Dinwiddie, the Lieutenant Governor of Virginia, placed George Washington at the head of a small band of colonial troops and gave them the task of building a road to the Monongahela River, near the spot where the French had constructed a stronghold called Fort Duquesne, located at the juncture of the Allegheny, Monongahela, and Ohio rivers (on the site of present-day Pittsburgh, Pennsylvania). Dinwiddie was worried about the growing French presence in the Ohio River Valley, which was then also claimed by the Colony of Virginia. Dinwiddie had also tried, and failed, to build a fort in the disputed region. At the Battle of Fort Necessity, in what is now western Pennsylvania, Washington was defeated in a skirmish with the French and their Indian allies. It was the future president's first military experience. The following year (1755), Gen. William Braddock, commander of His Majesty's British forces in North America, led an army of Regulars and Virginia Colonial Militia (which included Colonel Washington), on a march from Winchester, the seat of Frederick County, into the Ohio River country, in an unsuccessful attempt to dislodge the French from Fort Duquesne. The Battle of the Monongahela, which cost Braddock his life, marked the beginning of a conflict that the Americans called the French and Indian War (known in Europe as the "Seven Years War" since it did not officially begin until 1756). Of course, if Samuel Haycraft had caught a glimpse of Washington or Braddock and their men at this time, it is doubtful he would have remembered it later, considering that he was but two or three years old when all this happened.

By the time that Samuel Haycraft came of age the French had been decisively defeated in battle at Montreal, Quebec, and other places. When a treaty ending the war was negotiated in Paris in 1763, King Louis XV ceded Canada and all the land west of the Appalachian Mountains as far as the Mississippi River to the British. In a separate treaty, the Spanish received a large tract called Louisiana, leaving the French with no possessions whatever on the continent of North America.

Although the French no longer presented an obstacle to colonial expansion in the west, in 1773 the Indians were still troublesome (*although it could also be said that from the Indians' perspective, it was the white people who were troublesome*), attacking colonists who were then exploring or moving into the northern parts of present-day West Virginia and Kentucky, not far from the place where Samuel Haycraft had grown up. On June 9, 1774, the *Virginia Gazette* reported the Indians' intention to prosecute a full-fledged war against the colonists:

> An express arrived in Town [Williamsburg] last night from Pittsburg, with Letters to his Excellency the Governour from

Captain Connelly, Commandant at that Place; giving an Account that the Shawanese [Shawnee] Indians have openly declared their Intention of going to War with the white People, to revenge the Loss of some of their Nation who have been killed; that they had scalped one of the Traders, and detained all the rest who were in their Towns; that it was expected the Cherokees would join them, as they had sent a [wampum] Belt last Fall to the Northern Nations to strike the white People, which had been received by the Shawanese and Waabath [Wabash] Indians; that the Six Nations postponed their Answer till this Spring; and that there is soon to be a grand Council in the lower Shawanese Town, where about seventy Cherokees and a Number of other Indians are to attend, on the Subject of going to War with the English-Sundry Parties are now gone out, by Order of Captain Connelly, for the protection of the Inhabitants, and are to assemble at the Mouth of Whaling Creek, in Order, if it is judged practicable, to go against the upper Shawanese Town.-The Delawares, who profess to be our Friends, informed Captain Connelly that a Party of Shawanese were now gone against the Settlement; and it is imagined that they will fall upon Green Brier-All the Country about Pittsburg is in a very ruinous and discredited Situation, the Inhabitants having chiefly fled, and forted themselves as low as Old Town on Potowmack [Potomac] River.[4]

Hard on the heels of this news and reports of actual Indian attacks in July, Virginia's royal governor, Lord Dunmore, called out the militia. Among the many area settlers who answered the call to arms was twenty-one-year-old Samuel Haycraft, who enlisted as a private in Capt. William McMachen's company—a body of men that

---

[4] The Virginia Gazette, Williamsburg, Virginia, June 9, 1774.

consisted of three officers (a captain, a lieutenant, and an ensign), three non-commissioned officers (all sergeants), and thirty-two privates. One of the sergeants was reportedly named John Haycroft (but this is probably a mistake on the part of the person who transcribed the original records, more likely this is either James or Joshua, not John). Another one of my maternal ancestors, Thomas Gilliland, joined Capt. Michael Cresap's company as a private. Both Haycraft and Gilliland were on the pay roll at Pittsburgh (Fort Pitt).[5]

The only large-scale encounter of this brief conflict (it was over in a matter of months), which is remembered as "Lord Dunmore's War," was a victory for the Virginia colonial militia. Known as the Battle of Kanawha or Point Pleasant, this clash between colonial militia and Shawnee and Mingo Indians, led by a chief called Cornstalk, took place in what is now the state of West Virginia on October 10, 1774. Unfortunately, owing to incomplete records, it is difficult to ascertain the extent of Samuel Haycraft's participation in this war. It does not appear, however, that he took part in its most decisive battle.

Precisely what Samuel Haycraft was doing between the time he was released from John Neville's guardianship in 1773 and the outbreak of the American Revolution, apart from his brief service in the Virginia colonial militia during Dunmore's War, is equally difficult to ascertain. He may

---

[5] Lloyd DeWitt Bockstruck, *Virginia's Colonial Soldiers* (Baltimore, Maryland: Genealogical Publishing Company, 1988), 141-2.

have worked as a laborer for some farmer or plantation owner, or perhaps he was apprenticed to learn a trade. Unfortunately, we can only speculate and one guess is just as good as another.

One thing is certain: On April 19, 1775, the first shots of the American Revolution were fired at Lexington and Concord, Massachusetts. Shortly afterwards, the Continental Congress, to which George Washington was a delegate, convened in Philadelphia and among other things formed a Continental Army with Washington as its leader. The various colonies, including Virginia, also called for men to come to the aid of the Patriot cause and "in the latter part of the winter of 1775 or the fore part of the year 1776," Samuel Haycraft once more offered his services, enlisting this time for a term of two years and six months as a private in Capt. James Hook's company, 13th Virginia Regiment, under the command of Col. John Gibson.[6]

Samuel Haycraft's Revolutionary War pension file papers, combined with muster rolls that have survived to the present day, reveal that although some companies of the 13th Virginia took part in the battles at Brandywine and Germantown (and also suffered through the winter of 1777-1778 at Valley Forge), he was stationed "on the Frontier,"[7] where for most of the young soldier's term of service

---

[6] Samuel Haycraft Revolutionary War service record and Samuel Haycraft and Margaret Van Meter Haycraft Revolutionary War pension file, National Archives, Washington, D.C.
[7] Ibid.

Hook's company formed part of the garrison at Fort Pitt, where today only a stone and brick blockhouse, built in 1764, still stands to remind the citizens of Pittsburgh, Pennsylvania of the origins of their city.

Fort Pitt, named for British Prime Minister William Pitt, lay at the tip of a triangular point of land, where the waters of the Allegheny and Monongahela rivers flow together to create the Ohio River. It was here, at the so-called "Forks of the Ohio," in 1753, that the French first built a wooden stockade called Fort Duquesne, to bolster their claim to the Ohio River country. Five years later, during the French and Indian War, the French burned Fort Duquesne and then abandoned the site upon the approach of a superior British force. Between 1759 and 1761, at a cost of about £60,000, British soldiers constructed the solid five-pointed, star-shaped fort that Samuel Haycraft came to know well during the Revolutionary War after it fell into the hands of the State of Virginia. It is quite possible however, and even likely, that Samuel actually first saw the fort during his brief service in Lord Dunmore's War in 1774. In any event, here is a description of it:

> The earth around the proposed work was dug and thrown up so as to enclose the selected position with a rampart of earth. On the two sides facing the country, this rampart was supported by what military men call a revetment,—a brick work, nearly perpendicular, supporting the rampart on the outside, and thus preventing an obstacle to the enemy not easily overcome. On the other three sides, the earth in the rampart had no support,

and of course, it presented a more inclined surface to the enemy-one which could readily be ascended. To remedy, in some degree, this defect in the work, a line of pickets was fixed on the outside of the foot of the slope of the rampart. Around the whole work was a wide ditch which would, of course, be filled with water when the river was at a moderate stage.[8]

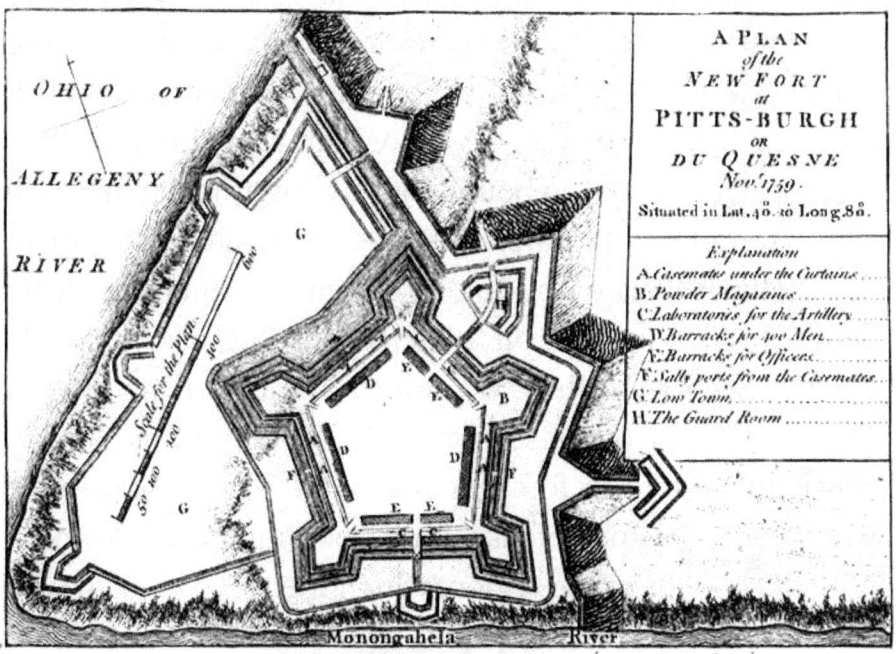

A plan of Fort Pitt or Duquesne, in 1765.

In 1772, three years prior to the start of the American Revolution, the British army abandoned Fort Pitt. The following year, "it was re-occupied and repaired by Dr. John Connelly, under orders from Lord Dunmore, Governor of

---

[8] Neville B. Craig, *The History of Pittsburgh* (Pittsburgh, Pennsylvania: John H. Mellor, 1851), 85-6.

Virginia."⁹ In 1774 the governor used it as a staging point for an attack on the Indians during the war that bears his name. (During that time, the governor's name was also temporarily attached to the Fort.) Interestingly, it was Samuel Haycraft's former guardian, John Neville, at the time a captain in the Virginia Militia, who in August 1775 led approximately "one hundred armed men" from Winchester to Fort Pitt to take permanent possession of the deserted fort for the colony of Virginia, which it claimed was located within the boundaries of Augusta County. This action reportedly "created quite a considerable excitement" among the leaders of the colony of Pennsylvania, which also claimed the territory on which Fort Pitt was located.¹⁰ Neville, who was afterward commissioned a general in the Continental Army, also served on a committee for the district in which the fort was situated, the purpose of which was to prepare for defense and if possible, to make peace with the Indians of the region, which was done in 1776 when Neville met at Fort Pitt with a chief named *Kiashuta* and several other chiefs, promising that the Americans would not "march an army through" Indian land "unless we hear of a British army coming this course; in such case we must make all haste to march and endeavor to stop them." Jacob Van Meter, Samuel Haycraft's future father-in-law (and another one of my ancestors, consequently), who then

---

[9] Ibid., 111.
[10] Ibid., 122.

resided near Garrard's Fort in what is now Greene County, Pennsylvania, also served on this committee.[11]

As the Revolutionary War progressed, "Fort Pitt seems to have risen in importance in the estimation of Congress, and demanded a more imposing force for its defence than the command of Major Neville." Consequently, General Lachlan McIntosh, with portions of the 8th Regiment of Pennsylvania and 13th of Virginia, were ordered there,"[12] which brings us back to Samuel Haycraft.

A view of the interior of Fort Pitt during the American Revolution; from *The Common School Catalogue* (1906).

---

[11] Ibid., 128 & 138-9.
[12] Ibid., 149.

Somehow, during the time he was helping to guard the frontier at Fort Pitt, Samuel Haycraft happened to meet eighteen-year-old Margaret Van Meter (also spelled Van Metre, Vanmeter, etc.), daughter of a former Frederick County, Virginia colonist named Jacob Van Meter, who in the late 1760s or early 1770s had taken up residence in what was then called the "Ten Mile Country," on land that was then being claimed by both Virginia and Pennsylvania. Perhaps they first saw one another when Margaret, also known as "Peggy," accompanied her father to Fort Pitt on business of some sort. In any event, the two young people met (Samuel was then only twenty-six), fell in love, and on September 9, 1778, they were married at Fort Pitt "by a Baptist Preacher by the name of John Corbly," with Samuel reportedly wearing his uniform. Afterward, Margaret later testified, she and Samuel lived together at Pittsburg-the frontier settlement established in 1760 outside the walls of the fort, until her husband was discharged upon the expiration of his term of service, August 2, 1779[13] (which means he probably enlisted in February 1776, which is close to the time he later remembered).

Later in life, when Samuel Haycraft applied for a federal pension based on his Revolutionary War service, certain individuals signed affidavits attesting to its veracity. One

---

[13] Samuel Haycraft Revolutionary War service record and Samuel Haycraft and Margaret Van Meter Haycraft Revolutionary War pension file, National Archives, Washington, D.C.
[13] Ibid.

was his brother-in-law Isaac Van Meter, who remembered that Samuel had also been stationed, for several months after his marriage, at a log stockade called Fort Laurens, located on the Tuscarawas River in what is now the state of Ohio. Named for Henry Laurens of South Carolina, President of the Continental Congress, the fort was built in 1778 by Gen. Lachlan McIntosh, to serve as a "stepping stone" for an attack on the British garrison at Fort Detroit, in present-day Michigan.[14] Van Meter also recalled that his brother-in-law often spoke "of the hunger and hardships he suffered at that post [Fort Laurens] and that he also complained that he "never had received his arrears of pay for his service and clothing and back rations." George Bruce, a fellow veteran, corroborated Van Meter's testimony, recalling that "in the later part of the year 1778 and part of 1779" Samuel Haycraft had been "stationed on the Tuskaraway [sic] River at Fort Laurance [sic], in a light infantry company led by Capt. Thomas More, and that during that time, the soldiers had been "reduced almost the whole of the winter on half allowance of flour and meat." Bruce remarked too that "for a considerable time" the garrison had been "surrounded by a large company of Indians who prevented us from getting a supply of provisions."[15]

---

[14] Samuel Hazard, *Pennsylvania Archives*, Vol. VII (Philadelphia, Pennsylvania: Joseph Severns & Company, 1853), 560.

[15] Samuel Haycraft Revolutionary War service record and Samuel Haycraft and Margaret Van Meter

The story of Fort Laurens, the only American fort to be built in the Ohio country during the Revolution, is well documented (although seldom if ever mentioned, even as a footnote, in U.S. History textbooks). Throughout the war, the British encouraged several tribes in what is the state of Ohio to attack colonial settlements. In consequence of this situation, in 1778 General McIntosh planned a "formidable incursion into the Indian country" in order to "destroy their towns and crops." Before doing so, he had a "a regular stockaded work, with four bastions and defended by six pieces of cannon" constructed at the confluence of the Ohio and Beaver rivers (in what is now the town of Beaver, Pennsylvania), about thirty-four miles north of Fort Pitt. The new stronghold was named Fort McIntosh.[16]

In September 1778, before marching into Indian country, McIntosh took the precaution of meeting at Fort Pitt with the Delawares, a friendly tribe, to "obtain their consent to the passing of troops through their territory." Then, in October, "Gen. McIntosh assembled one thousand men, at the newly erected fort, at the mouth of [the] Beaver, and commenced this expedition," which unfortunately, as one observer wrote, "seems to have been unproductive of any good effect."[17]

Haycraft Revolutionary War pension file, National Archives, Washington, D.C.
[16] Craig, 147-8.
[17] Ibid., 148.

The season was so far advanced that the army only proceeded about seventy miles west of Fort McIntosh and halted on the west bank of the Tuskarawas river, a little below the mouth of Sandy creek. Here they built a fort on an elevated piece of ground and named it Fort Laurens. Colonel John Gibson was left in the fort with one hundred and fifty men, and the army returned to Fort Pitt.[18]

One of these one hundred and fifty men (another source says there were one hundred and eighty) was Samuel Haycraft, who also almost certainly took part in the construction of Fort Laurens, which was recollected many years later by John Cuppy, another veteran of the expedition:

> Where Fort Laurens was built, [there] was no timber, on a high bank, and a barren back for half a mile or more; and the men had to carry in the timber, four or five to a stick. Made mostly of large, hard-wood timber, split, some six inches thick, bullet proof, planted in trenches three feet deep, solidly packed around, and extending fifteen feet above ground...the fort, which was on the west bank of the Tuscarawas, enclosed about an acre of ground and was the longest on the river. No pickets along the river bank, no high overlooking ground either near Fort McIntosh or Laurens. The gate was on the west side of the fort, no spring; relied upon the river for supply of water. There was one block-house, about 20 feet square, which was directly to the right of the gate, and next to it, and formed a part of the outside in place of picketing: the block-house, about six feet above the ground, the block-house was made a foot wider on the

---

[18] Ibid.

wall side, and made to over-jut, so if Indians came up, the garrison could shoot down through this open jut directly upon an enemy below; and the floor of puncheons on a level with the over-jut; and the timbers built up some eight feet, so as to completely protect those within from the enemy without, and port-holes all around about five feet from the floor, and some two or three feet apart, through to which for the garrison to fire in case of any attack, with a rude roof slanting one way and that within the fort...There were also 2 cabins built on each end of the fort, not quite together and in a line with the picketing, and helped to form the enclosure, and also had over-jutting, and with port-holes; but smaller than the block-house; and these were for shelter and provision.[19]

During the building of the fort, before Samuel Haycraft and some 150 of his comrades were left behind, the army was "encamped in the open ground in a semi-circle around Fort Laurens, some distance from the fort, but not so far back as the woods, in tents; every mess, composed of six or seven men, had a tent." All their baggage, Cuppy recalled "was packed on horses."[20]

Throughout this time, Cuppy likewise remembered, the "Indians were entirely peaceable" Not only were there "no attacks from them," he said, but they "frequently visited the camp, and brought fine fat haunches of venison, bear meat and turkies, and presented [them] to the officers, who gave them some of their too beloved fire-water in return."

---

[19] Louise Phelps Kellogg, Ed., *Wisconsin Historical Collections, Volume XXIII, Draper Series, Vol. IV, Frontier Advance on the Upper Ohio, 1778-1779* (Madison, Wisconsin: Wisconsin Historical Society, 1916), 159-60.
[20] Ibid., 160.

SKETCH OF FORT LAURENS ON THE TUSCARAWAS—NAMES OF OTHER FORTS IN OHIO, &c., &c.

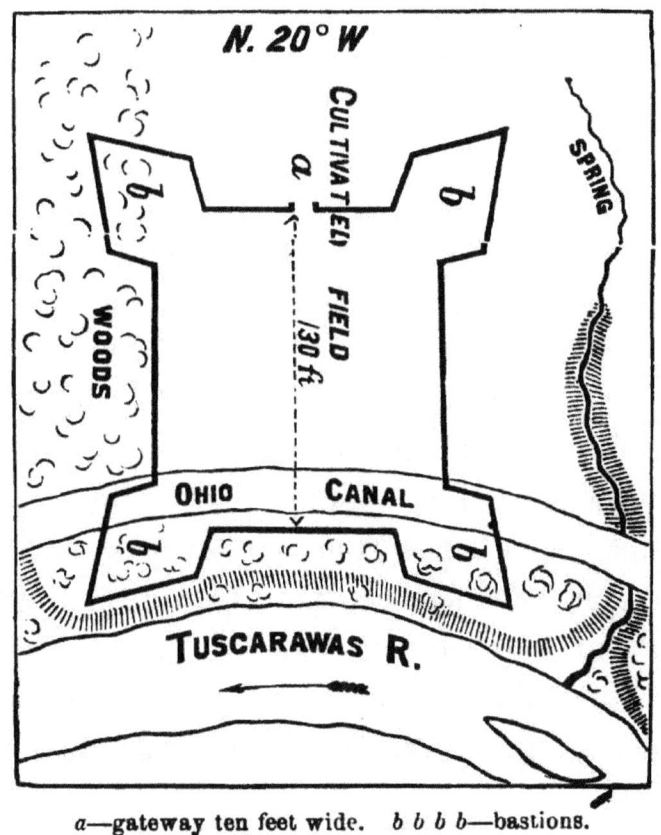

a—gateway ten feet wide.   *b b b b*—bastions.

From *Annals of Ohio, Historic Events* (1876).

The former soldier also recollected seeing the Indians, "both men and women," dancing "a hundred or more together, the taller taking the lead, and others falling into the circle, according to their height, the shortest bringing up the rear, and dancing around in the circle, to the rude music derived from beating upon a kettle by an old Indian, intermingled with occasional yells." Cuppy also remembered that Simon Girty, a Scots-Irish frontiersman that lived among the Indians, was present.[21] Girty, who at the outset of the war was a friend to the Americans, afterward turned against them.

Informed of McIntosh's expedition, Gen. George Washington made it clear that he considered both Fort Laurens and Fort McIntosh to be "material posts." He was particularly anxious that Laurens, most probably due to its distance from any other fort, "be sufficiently garrisoned and…well supplied with provision that it may not be liable to fall through want in case of attack."[22] Unfortunately, that is not what happened. In January 1779, when hostile Indians learned that the soldiers in the fort were not only few in number but also short on supplies, they decided to take advantage of the situation. Here is a description of the subsequent siege of Fort Laurens, according to one account:

> The first hostile demonstration of the forest warriors was executed with equal cunning and success. The horses of the garrison were allowed to forage for themselves upon herbage, among the prairie grass in the immediate vicinity of the fort-wearing bells, that they might be the more easily found if

---

[21] Ibid.
[22] George Washington to Daniel Brodhead, May 3, 1779, the George Washington Papers at the Library of Congress, 1741-1799 [https://www.loc.gov/collections/george-washington-papers/; Accessed March 1, 2012}.

straying too far. It happened one morning in January that the horses had all disappeared, but the bells were heard at no great distance. They had, in truth, been stolen by the Indians and conveyed away. The bells, however, were taken off, and used for another purpose. Availing themselves of the tall prairie grass, the Indians formed an ambuscade, at the farthest extremity of which they caused the bells to jingle as a decoy. The artifice was successful. Sixteen men were sent in pursuit of the straggling steeds, who fell into the snare. Fourteen were killed upon the spot and remaining two taken prisoners; of these latter, one of whom returned at the close of the war, and of the other nothing was ever heard.

Toward evening of the same day, the whole force of the Indians, painted, and in full costume of war, presented themselves in full view of the garrison, by marching in single files, though at a respectful distance, across the prairie. Their number, according to a count from one of the bastions, was eight hundred and forty-seven—altogether too great to be encountered in the field by so small a garrison. After this display of their strength, the Indians took a position upon an elevated piece of ground at no great distance from the fort, though on the opposite side of the river. In this situation they remained several weeks, in a state of armed neutrality than of active hostility. Some of them would frequently approach the fort sufficiently near to hold conversations with those upon the walls. They uniformly professed a desire for peace, but protested against the encroachments of the white people upon their lands—more especially was the erection of a fort so far within the territory claimed by them as exclusively their own, a cause of complaint-nay, of admitted exasperation. There was with the Americans in the fort, an aged friendly Indian named John Thompson, who seemed to be in equal favor with both parties, visiting the Indian encampment at pleasure, and coming and going as he chose. They informed Thompson that they deplored the continuance of hostilities, and finally sent word by him to Colonel Gibson, that they were desirous of peace, and if he would present them with a barrel of flour, they would send in their proposals the next day. The flour was sent, but the Indians, instead of fulfilling their part of the stipulation, withdrew, and entirely disappeared. They had, indeed, continued the siege as long as they could obtain subsistence, and raised it only because of the lack of supplies. Still, as the beleaguerment was begun in stratagem, so was it ended.[23]

Some accounts of this episode report that a small contingent of British soldiers under the command of Captain Henry Bird also took part in the siege of Fort Laurens. "However," states one source, "it would appear that he remained at Sandusky, directing the raids [against the Americans], and watching to prevent the anticipated American march against Detroit."[24]

Shortly after the apparent withdrawal of the Indians, Colonel Gibson, worried that his "provisions were...running short," sent "a detachment of fifteen men" led by "Colonel Clark, of the Pennsylvania line" to Fort McIntosh, as an escort for "the invalids of the garrison." The move turned out to be unwise because unknown to Gibson, "the Indians had left a strong party of observation lurking in the neighborhood of the fort."[25] Consequently, "the escort had proceeded only two miles before it was fallen upon, and

---

[23] William L. Stone, *Life of Joseph Brant (Thayendanegea), including the Border Wars of the Revolution* (Albany, New York: J. Munsell, 1865), 396-7.
[24] Kellogg, 251.
[25] Stone, 398; Note: In a letter to Col. Archibald Lochley, dated January 29, 1779, in which he states the ambush took place about 3 miles from Fort Laurens, General McIntosh says only two men were killed and four were wounded and one taken prisoner, see Kellogg, 210.

the whole number killed with the exception of four-one of whom, a captain, escaped back to the fort." Afterward, "the bodies of the slain were interred by the garrison, on the same day, with the honors of war." Soldiers were also "sent out to collect the remains of the fourteen who had first fallen by the ambuscade, and bury them." No doubt to their horror, the burial party discovered that wolves had been eating the flesh of the dead soldiers. After interring their fallen comrades, the men set traps "upon the new-made graves." The next morning, "some of those ravenous beasts were caught and shot."[26]

Afterward, as Samuel Haycraft seems to have remembered for the rest of his life, the "situation of the garrison" became "deplorable." "For two weeks the men had been reduced to half a pound of sour flour, and like quantity of offensive meat, per diem; and for a week longer they were compelled to subsist only upon raw hides, and such roots as they could find in the circumjacent woods and prairies."[27] One man later recalled that near the end of the four-week-long siege, the men "had to live on half a biscuit a day-then the last two days washed their moccasons [sic] and broiled them for food, and broiled strips of old dried hides." He also remembered that when two soldiers "stole

---

[26] Stone, 398.
[27] Ibid.

out and killed a deer" and then "returned with it, it was devoured in a few minutes, some not waiting to cook it."²⁸

Finally, General McIntosh "most opportunely arrived to their relief, with supplies and a reinforcement of seven hundred men." Unfortunately, due to "an untoward incident" that caused "the loss of a great portion of their fresh supplies," the soldiers "came near to being immediately reduced to short allowance again."²⁹

> These supplies were transported through the wilderness upon pack-horses. The garrison, overjoyed at the arrival of succors, on their approach to within about a hundred yards of the fort manned the parapets and fired a salute of musketry. But the horses must have been young in the service. Affrighted at the detonation of the guns, they began to rear and plunge, and broke from their guides. The example was contagious, and in a moment more, the whole cavalcade of pack-horses were bounding into the woods at full gallop, dashing their burdens to the ground and scattering them over many a rood in all directions-the greater portion of which could never be recovered. But there was yet enough of provisions saved to cause the mingling of evil with the good. Very incautiously, the officers dealt out two days' rations per man, the whole of which was devoured by the famishing soldiers, to the imminent hazard of the lives of all, and resulting in the severe sickness of many. Leaving the fort again, General M'Intosh assigned the command to Major Vernon, who remained upon the station several months. He, in turn, was left to endure the horrors of famine, until longer to endure was death; whereupon the fort was evacuated and the position abandoned-its occupation and

---

[28] Kellogg, 257.
[29] Stone, 398.

maintenance, at the cost of great fatigue and suffering, and the expense of many lives, having been of not the least service to the country.[30]

During the siege of Fort Laurens, Col. Daniel Brodhead wrote to General Washington from Fort Pitt to inform him that General McIntosh "is unfortunate enough to be almost universally Hated by every man in this department, both Civil and Military." Adding that he did not think it was possible for McIntosh to "do any thing Salutary," Brodhead added: "There is not an Officer who does not appear to be exceedingly disgusted, and I am much deceived if they serve under his immediate Command another Campaign."[31] Considering the suffering they had been made to endure and the loss of several of their comrades' lives for no apparent good reason, enlisted men like Samuel Haycraft almost certainly felt the same way. In light of this seemingly universal opinion and also because McIntosh had reportedly asked to be relieved of command, the Continental Congress passed a resolution on February 20, 1779, recalling him and permitting General Washington to appoint Brodhead as his replacement.

---

[30] Ibid., 398-9.
[31] George Washington Papers, Series 4, General Correspondence: Daniel Brodhead to George Washington, January 16, 1779, George Washington Papers at the Library of Congress, Washington, D.C.

It is also not hard to imagine that upon Samuel Haycraft's return to Fort Pitt on April 7, 1779,[32] his young wife greeted him with tears of joy and relief that he had survived an ordeal that had proved so deadly to others.

****

There are three extant Revolutionary War muster rolls in the National Archives with Samuel Haycraft's name on them. The oldest is dated March 17, 1778, showing him present at Fort Pitt as a member of Captain Russell's company. The second, covering the months of April and May 1779, records his presence at Fort Pitt as a member of Captain Springer's company. The final roll, which shows him present at Fort Pitt as a member of Lt. Ephraim Ralph's company, in the newly designated 9th Virginia Regiment, is for July, August, and September 1779. (Note: On May 12, 1779, the 13th was reorganized as the 9th Virginia Regiment.) This third muster roll also shows, following what was hopefully a relatively uneventful four months after his return from Fort Laurens, that Samuel Haycraft was discharged upon the expiration of his term of service on August 2, 1779.[33]

---

[32]

[33] Samuel Haycraft Revolutionary War service record, National Archives, Washington, D.C.

Only days after he was discharged, Samuel and his bride joined a flotilla of rafts, bearing about a hundred people, including Margaret's parents and siblings, and set off down the Ohio River to an inland region that was then called "Kaintuck." Upon arrival, Samuel and Margaret, along with the Van Meter family and others, traveled overland to the Severns Valley, where they became the founders of Hardin County, Kentucky, and its seat, Elizabethtown, with Samuel Haycraft as one of its leading citizens. In his later years he served as a Kentucky state representative and also, in 1812, as a presidential elector, voting for James Madison and running mate Elbridge Gerry, who with Samuel's help and that of 127 other electors, won a second term of office.

Samuel Haycraft, Sr. died on October 15, 1823 at the age of seventy. He was buried at the city cemetery in Elizabethtown, where his widow, Margaret, joined him twenty years later. In the summer of 2012, while on a road trip, I traveled to Elizabethtown, where I saw their graves. I also visited the site of Fort Pitt, at the confluence of the Allegheny and Monongahela Rivers, where the great city of Pittsburgh stands today. I've not yet visited the site of Fort Laurens, but I hope to do so someday.

Five years later, I went on another road trip, one that took me through Savannah, Georgia, among many other places in the South. There, in Savannah, entirely by chance, I happened upon the graves of Col. Lachlan McIntosh and his great-nephew, James, while strolling through Colonial

Park Cemetery, where they are buried. Each of the McIntoshs has a Georgia historical marker next to his tomb, which is what called my attention to them. Naturally, I could not help but think, while gazing upon them, how Colonel McIntosh's incompetency and the building of his so-called "stepping stone" had nearly spelled the doom of my ancestor, Samuel Haycraft, and how, if he had starved to death at Fort Laurens in 1779, I would never have been born! It just goes to show how slender a thread our very existence can sometimes depend upon.

The Last Battle of the Revolution

If you were to ask anyone who has ever taken an American History course in high school or college to name the last battle of the American Revolution, chances are, if they didn't say, "I don't know," they might answer: "Yorktown," because that's what they've been taught. And yes, it's true that the Battle of Yorktown, Virginia, which in October 1781 pitted the combined Franco-American forces of Gen. George Washington and Count Rochambeau against a British army led by Gen. Lord Cornwallis *was* the last *major* armed contest of the Revolution. It can also be said that it was the *most decisive*. However, it was *not* the last battle, which as it happens, or rather *happened*, took place *not* in Tidewater Virginia as most people think, but rather, in the so-called "backcountry," at a place called Fort Henry, in what is now the state of West Virginia. It's likewise a fact that among the fort's defenders was one of my collateral ancestors—a son of Conrad Wheat—which explains how I found out about it.

****

Remember Conrad Wheat? The man whose home was invaded and his grandchild kidnapped in an incident described in the chapter entitled "The Malevolent Magistrate?" Well, in 1767, two years after the so-called "riot" at his home occurred, he decided to move. (As I wrote in the aforementioned chapter, who can blame him, with a landlord like Evan Shelby!) Where did he go? The answer is Air Township, Cumberland County, Pennsylvania, about sixty-five miles north of Frederick County, Maryland, where in March 1767 he received a grant of 300 acres. But apparently, Conrad was a restless man, and the West beckoned. By 1774, he had moved again, this time nearly 300 miles west to Ohio County, Virginia (now West Virginia), where he settled on 400 acres of land that was formally granted to him on February 23, 1780. This land was located on the east side of the Ohio River, within the limits of the present-day city of Wheeling, West Virginia.

Apart from the grant, a copy of which is in the land survey records of Ohio County, Conrad Wheat's presence in the area is also confirmed by his signature on a "Memorial of the Inhabitants of the Country West of the Alleghany Mountains" to form a new state, to be called Westsylvania,[1] which clearly the Continental Congress did not approve since West Virginia did not become a state until 1863 and it wasn't called "Westsylvania." (See Appendix.)

---

[1] Howard L. Leckey, *The Ten-Mile Country and Its Pioneers* (Baltimore, Maryland: Clearfield Company, Inc., 2001), 148.

A roster or muster roll of "Soldiers who took the oath of allegiance to the Commonwealth of Virginia in Ohio County in 1777" further confirms Conrad Wheat's presence in Ohio County, as well as his status as a combatant in the American Revolution, Dated September 4, 1777, this roster was compiled by a neighbor named Andrew Caldwell. The name of Conrad Wheat, Jr. is found on a similar roll drawn up by one Silas Hedges on September 24, 1777.[2]

If my own experience is typical, and I think it probably is, most Americans are taught little or nothing about the events that took place in the West, or "backcountry," during the American Revolution, such as the expedition of George Rogers Clarke. Thus, something important is either downplayed or overlooked entirely. It's true that frontier battles, in which Americans were usually fighting more Indians than British troops, were not as large in terms of numbers, nor singularly as consequential as contests that took place in the east, such as Saratoga—which convinced the King of France, Louis XVI, to provide financial and military aid to the fledgling United States—or the Battle of Yorktown—which led Britain to question whether continuing to try to put down a rebellion was worth the effort. Nevertheless, without American victories on the frontier, it's arguable as to how willing the British government might have been to concede the Trans

---

[2] Howard L. Lecky, *The Ten-Mile Country and Its Pioneers* (1950), 139.

Appalachian West—that vast territory that lay between the Appalachian Mountains and Mississippi River—as well as the Northwest Territory, to the United States when the 1783 Treaty of Paris was negotiated. It is a fundamental tenet that "possession is nine-tenths of the law," which means that in property disputes, the law favors whoever is in actual possession of the property and exercising control over it, which is what Americans, by and large, were doing in the West when the U.S. and Britain entered into peace negotiations in 1782. Knowing that my ancestor, Conrad Wheat, and also his son, Conrad, Jr., were Patriots who not only took part in the struggle for independence but also helped assure the territorial enlargement of the then-new United States, is gratifying to me.

Unfortunately, apart from being mustered into service in 1775, practically nothing else is known about Conrad Wheat's military service during the American Revolution, but here's what I *do* know: In 1774, the same year that my ancestor settled in Ohio County, Virginia, a log stockade called Fort Fincastle was built on the east bank of the Ohio River, in the middle of what is now downtown Wheeling, West Virginia. It was located not very far from the home he had carved out of the wilderness for himself and his family. The fort, rectangular in shape from all accounts, with a blockhouse at each corner, was named for Viscount Fincastle or Lord Dunmore, who was then the royal colonial governor of Virginia. Its purpose was to provide protection to settlers living on the edge of what was then the frontier, where they were exposed to raids by Native Americans that objected to their presence. After the Revolution began, and Governor Dunmore overthrown, the fort was renamed for his successor, Patrick Henry, who is perhaps most famous for saying, "Give me liberty or give me death!" (He was lucky. He got liberty.)

During the Revolution the fort was attacked twice. The first time in 1777 and the second time in 1782. Although I do not know for sure, I want to believe that Conrad was present on the first occasion, which was described in an early nineteenth century magazine:

> The first assault was in Sept. 1777; when it was attacked by 380 Indians, headed by the notorious Simon Girty. Col. Zane, with thirty-three men, assisted by the women, several of whom stood by the sides of their husbands or lovers, and discharged their rifles with fearless intrepidity. Amongst the females was Betsy Wheat, a young woman of German extraction: when Girty urged the garrison to surrender, promising quarters, &c., and there was a parley among the men, as to what was best to be done, Betsy answered Girty with all the keenness of female irony, shamed such of the men as seemed disposed to surrender, and infused fresh courage into the disheartened garrison. The siege was continued for twenty-four hours, during which time the Indians kept up a constant fire. Seeing no prospect of success, and fearing an attack themselves from the neighboring garrisons, they retreated, after destroying nearly three hundred head of cattle, horses, and hogs, and burning the houses in the village, then amounting to about twenty-five dwellings. The consequent distress of the inhabitants was very great, as most of them lost not only their furniture and provisions, but all their

clothing, excepting what they had on: the suddenness of the attack giving them no time to remove any thing to the fort but their own persons. In this siege some the garrison were wounded, but none killed; the main loss fell on a reconnoitering party, who, having gone out early one morning, were ambushed by the Indians, and twenty-three of the number killed in sight of the fort. The loss sustained by the savages was never certainly known.[3]

It appears that Conrad Wheat died sometime shortly after March 14, 1781, the date on which he drew up his will. At the time of his demise, he was sixty-three-years-old, which was considered elderly in those days. Consequently, he was not present at Fort Henry when Native Americans and British rangers attacked a second time. The battle that followed is significant. Why? Because most people think that the Battle of Yorktown, which ended on October 19, 1781 with a victory by the combined forces of George Washington and Count Rochambeau over Lord Cornwallis was the last battle of the Revolution, but it *wasn't*. The last battle of the Revolution was in fact the Second Battle of Fort Henry, in which its defenders emerged victorious in September 1782.

In a book entitled *History of the Early Settlements and Indian Wars of Western Virginia*, published in 1851, the author, Wills De Hass, lists the names of twenty-seven defenders of the fort that he "with great pains collected."

---

[3] *The American Journal of Science and Arts*, Vol. XXXI, January 1837, 4.

Unfortunately, he does not identify any of his sources. Nevertheless, among these names can be found "Conrad Wheat and four sons." This is not the mistake which at first glance it appears to be. The list refers to my sixth great-granduncle, Conrad Wheat, *Junior*, who was also sometimes referred to as Conrad Wheat, Senior, since he too had a son named Conrad Wheat—one of the four to which De Hass referred in his book!

De Hass also identifies a woman named Betsy Wheat as being inside the fort when it was attacked. Who was she? Well, she wasn't Conrad Sr.'s widow, whose name was Margaret, and she wasn't one of his daughters, who were Catherine—the one whose "bastard child" was the cause of the 1765 "riot" at Wheat's home in Frederick County, Maryland—or Molly, who had married a man named Wendel Coons, given birth in 1773 to a son named Martin and then died, apparently, sometime before 1781. It is generally believed, since there is no other possible explanation, that Betsy Wheat was Conrad Jr.'s wife, who De Hass and others credit with helping defend the fort.

De Hass' account of the second battle of Fort Henry, published in 1851, appears to be the earliest ever published. There have been many others since then. The ones I like best, however, appeared in two rival Wheeling, West Virginia newspapers on the occasion of the one-hundredth anniversary of the 1782 battle. I've included substantial portions of both in this chapter because though each is packed with information, there are some things that one mentions that the other does not. As was customary at the time, each one refers to the Native Americans attackers as "savages," an offensive term that has since fallen out of use.

The first of these narratives, which appeared in a newspaper called *The Intelligencer*, provides a history and description of Fort Henry as well as the forces that besieged it. Published on September 12, 1882, it pre-dates the other account by only a few days.

> Originally called Fort Fincastle in honor of Lord Dunmore, who at the time of its erection was Governor of the colony, in the year 1776 its name was changed to Fort Henry, in honor of Patrick Henry, the first Governor of the Commonwealth. It was erected in the year 1774, the immediate cause of its erection being found in the fact that an apprehended attack from the savages during the year was anticipated, and a place of defense for the protection of the infant settlement, of which they were destitute, was demanded. It was planned by General George Rogers Clark, Commandant of the Western Military Department, and was built by the settlers.
> In shape it was a parallelogram, being about three hundred and fifty-six feet in length and about one hundred and fifty feet in width, and was surrounded by pickets about twelve feet high, with bastions at each corner. Inside of the stockade cabins were erected for the shelter of such as sought its protection, a magazine for military stores, a block house, the second story of which projected over the lower, filled with port holes, through which the trusty rifle of the pioneer sent its death-dealing missile. On the top of the block house was a mounted swivel, a four-pounder, which did effective work in an emergency. Wells were also sunk in the inclosure, so that a supply of water was secured at all times.

To the south-east, and about fifty yards distant from the fort, stood the residence of Col. Ebenezer Zane—a cabin built of rough-hewn logs, with a kitchen or outbuilding in the rear, which also had attached to a magazine for military stores.

FORT HENRY.—1777.
From *History and Government of West Virginia* (1896).

This house served as an outpost during the last siege of the fort, which occurred on the 11th day of September, 1782, and contributed greatly to the defeat of the Indians and their British allies on that memorable occasion. There were two regular sieges of the fort—the one in the year 1777 and the other in the year 1782, both of which were successfully repulsed. At the last siege the Indians were commanded by James Girty and the British troops by Capt. Pratt. Many writers name Simon Girty as the one in command on this occasion, but this is a mistake, as at this time he was with an Indian army which had invaded the territory of Kentucky, and he was present at its attack on Bryant's Station, which occurred but a short time prior to the attack on Fort Henry.

James Girty was even more vindictive and bloodthirsty than his brother Simon Girty, but was not so conspicuous a character as the latter. There is reason to believe, however, that many of the atrocious deeds attributed to Simon Girty, the recital of which even at this late date makes the blood to run cold with horror, were perpetrated by James.

On the happening of the last siege the settlers on short and sudden notice had barely time to escape to the shelter of the fort, so unexpected was the appearance of the savages, consequently their homes, together with their furniture, were left exposed to the rapacity and cupidity of their assailants. It was towards evening that the Indian forces with their allies appeared, and from that time until midnight, repeated and furious assaults were made by them on the inmates, which were as often repulsed.

When the attack began, Col. Ebenezer Zane and some other settlers remained in the lone blockhouse adjacent to Zane's house while most others ran for the fort. I particularly like the second newspaper account, which follows, because it is couched in the sort of colorful language that is rarely used in story-telling anymore. It was published in the *Wheeling Sunday Register* on September 17, 1882, following a centennial commemoration of the battle by the citizens of Wheeling, West Virginia. For all intents and purposes, this version of the story begins with reference to Col. Zane, whose sister, Elizabeth, is a notable figure in this, and all other, accounts. I point him out, dear reader, because this same, "Col. Zane" was mentioned by my ancestor, Conrad Wheat, Sr., in his will, in which he directed that his grandson Martin Coons' share of his estate be "deposited into the hands of Mr. Ebenezer Zane untill the said Martin Coons shall Arrive of Age to receive it." Martin Coons, by the way, was my 5th great-grandfather.

Here is the story of the 1782 attack on Fort Henry that appeared in the Wheeling *Sunday Register*:

> True to his former determination, Col. Zane remained there [in his blockhouse] during the siege, and with the aid and cooperation of those who remained with him, defended it with resolute valor and brave success. The names of those who remained with him and contributed to its defence were Andrew Scott, Geo. Green, Elizabeth, the wife of Colonel Zane, Molly Scott, Miss McCulloch, a sister of Mrs. Zane's, who at the time was visiting there, "Sam," a Guinea negro, and his wife, Kate, both of whom belonged to Col. Zane and were devotedly attached to him. Jonathan and Silas Zane and their sister Elizabeth, together with the settlers [which] had fled to the fort.
>
> But a brief time had elapsed after they had entered and closed the gates before the Indians made their appearance filing along the ravine, the head of which was just back of Col. Zane's house, in full view of the Fort, waving the British flag, under the folds of which they marched, and demanding in the name of his majesty, King George, the immediate and unconditional surrender of the house and the Fort. Silas Zane, who was in command of the stockade, replied to their imperious demand by ordering a young man who stood beside him to shoot down the color bearer, which was no sooner said than done, and that was the last time that British colors floated over the soil of West Virginia.
>
> Bold and defiant as this incident was on the part of the whites, it did not precipitate an immediate attack by assault upon the part of the savages, and only occasional random firing was kept up between the belligerents, when even this ceased as the darkness of night settled down upon the scene, which was

illuminated here and there by a few camp fires. Even these were permitted to expire and quiet and silence prevailed.

The whites, however, were not deluded by appearances and their vigilance was not permitted to sleep. They were equal to the tricks and stratagems of the savages, knowing full well that the quiet and silence under the circumstances boded no good. This was soon made evident, for about twelve o'clock they rushed hard on the pickets in order to storm, but were promptly repulsed. This was followed by two other attempts to storm before day, but to no purpose. About eight o'clock on the following morning, a negro deserter, who had hidden himself in one of the unoccupied cabins during the assaults made in the course of the previous night came running towards the Fort at the top of his speed, crying in pleading tones, "Open the gate— open the gate." The gate was opened and he was admitted. From him much valuable information was obtained concerning the designs and purposes of the Indians and their allies. Among other things he also reported the force to consist of two hundred and sixty Indians and forty British regulars, under the command of a British captain. The enemy kept up a continual firing during the second day, which was punctually replied to from Col. Zane's house and the fort. But the savages had learned to practice caution from their late experiences, and were loathe to expose themselves unnecessarily to the sure aim of the backwoodsmen, seeking cover behind favorable objects and shelter in the few abandoned cabins scattered around.

When the alarm was given by Lynn of this approach of the savages, the supply of powder provided by the settlers for their defence was deemed ample, but by reason of the protracted continuance of the savages and the repeated endeavors made by them to storm the forts, this supply on the afternoon of the second day was well nigh exhausted. It therefore became necessary for them to renew their stock from the abundance of the material in the house of Col. Zane. Hence it was proposed that one of their fleetest men should endeavor to reach the house, obtain a keg, and return with it to the fort.

The Last Battle of the Revolution

Notwithstanding it was an enterprise fraught with dangers, and almost certain death to the man who would undertake it, several young men promptly volunteered. At the same time a young female stepped forward and offered her services, sustaining the reasonableness of her offer with arguments convincing to her own mind and which finally proved to those around her. When told that a man would encounter less danger by reason of his greater fleetness, she replied: "And should he fall, his loss will be more severely felt. You have not one man to spare. A woman will not be missed in the defence of the fort."

This offer of Elizabeth Zane's was accepted. Divesting herself of such of her garments would have a tendency to impede her progress and casting aside her shoes and stockings, upon the gate being thrown open she bounded forth in all the energy of youth. The Indians, amazed at the unwonted appearance of a woman, made no attempt to interrupt her progress as she sprang forward, but indulged in the contemptuous exclamation of, "A squaw!" "A squaw!"

Having safely arrived at her brother's house, she hurriedly related her errand, whereupon Col. Zane fastened a table-cloth around her waist, and emptying into it a keg or powder, again she ventured forth.

But by this time the apprehensions of the Indians were aroused, and they ceased to remain passive and indifferent spectators. A volley of balls whistled around her, raising such a cloud of dust, that, as she afterwards remarked, was almost impossible for her to see her way before her. However, she succeeded in reaching the fort unharmed with her precious treasure and thereby secured its safety.

When intelligence reached Shepherd's Fort of the investiture of Fort Henry, a party of men left the former fort with a view of rending assistance in the latter, but on arriving in the vicinity of the fort they found that it would be impossible to gain admission, and thereupon determined to return. A son-in-law of Col. Shepherd's, Francis Duke by name, being one of the party, insisted, that if no one else would, he alone would make the attempt to gain ingress. All arguments to dissuade him from his purpose proved unavailing. He fully recognized the desperateness of the undertaking, but his chivalric nature and resolute spirit could not be curbed. Not regarding the danger attaching to so rash an enterprise, but subordinating this to the higher and nobler promptings of his unselfish nature, which led him alone to see the peril which menaced friends under the threatening and fearful circumstances by which they were encumbered and who needed every man they could secure, put spurs to his horse, and breaking through the Indian lines, rode towards the fort crying, "Open the gate! Open the gate!" He was recognized by those within the fort, and the gate swung open for his admission, but before reaching it he was pierced by the deadly bullets of the savage foe and fell a martyr to his gallant, daring and noble disinterestedness.

Foiled as the assailants had been in their assaults on the night of the first day, yet they did not wholly suspend their efforts. Col. Zane had arranged and posted the force in his house to the best advantage, and as the Indians made their desperate assault on the pickets during that night, he opened on them with a well directed fire, which contributed to their repulse in no small degree. Hence it became an important matter with them to get rid of this outpost, and accordingly after their vain assaults against the fort, they held a consultation, which resulted in a determination to make the attempt under the cover of night to destroy the house, the inmates of which had so seriously [word uncertain] them in their designs.

They concluded it must be held and reduced to ashes. After an interval, when silence had settled down upon the scene and it was presumed that the whites had in some degree relaxed their caution, a savage with a burning brand in his hand crawled to the vicinity of the kitchen of the house, and raising from the ground, waved the brand to and fro and then blowing his breath about it to rekindle it, proceeded to apply it to a pile of brush and wood he had placed against the logs of the building, when suddenly a shot rang out in the darkness and silence, and howling with rage and pain, the would be incendiary, with slow and hobbling gait, sought the deep cover of the darkness. The vigilant eye of watchful "Sam," the faithful negro, had detected him just in time to upset his well considered but poorly executed plans.

On the evening of the eleventh, not long after the appearance of the Indians, before the fort a perogue loaded with cannon balls, on its way from Fort Pitt to the falls of the Ohio, containing three men, was floating leisurely along with the current a short distance above the settlement, when their attention was attracted by the sound of firing in the direction of the Fort. Daniel Sullivan, who was in command of the boat, sent the other two men along the shore of the river, telling them to inform the inmates of the Fort that he was coming with a load of canon [sic] balls, and to be on the lookout for him. The man arrived safely and entered the postern gate unobserved by the savages. In a short time Sullivan arrived with his boat, but unfortunately he did not escape detection, for he was perceived by the Indians just as he landed and was compelled to abandon it and scramble up the bluff to reach the same gate through which his companions had successfully passed but a brief time before, But he was not so fortunate as they in escaping unhurt; for, as he was about entering the gate, he received a slight wound which was painful, although it was not serious.

On the afternoon of the second day (12th) after the feat performed by Elizabeth Zane, the Indians arrived at the resolution that they would put these cannon balls which had so opportunely fallen into their hands to use, by employing them in the demolition of the fortress.

The suggestion no sooner revealed itself to them that they commenced to carry it into execution. Obtaining a log, which they considered as being adapted to the purpose, they hollowed it out, and binding it with chains, which they obtained from a blacksmith shop in the vicinity, they charged it heavily with powder and rammed home a few of the captured balls, and placing it in position, pointing in the direction of the Fort, nothing doubting but what it would carry dismay and death in its course (as it did), made all things ready. A big Indian with a lighted match, advanced through a crowd of his companions, gathered to inspect this new engine of destruction, and to witness the effects of the discharge. A dreadful explosion followed—its pieces flew in all directions, and instead of being the cause of ruin to the fort, was the source of injury only to themselves; several were killed, many wounded, and all were terror stricken for the time, by the unlooked for result. Thus were they hoisted on their own petard.

But the finale of this episode served only to exasperate them and to render them more furious, and so when the curtain of night was drawn around the world they resolved, in the energy of their desperation, to make a final effort for the reduction of the fort.

Filled with that frenzy produced by defeat, about two o'clock on the night of the 12th, they made another attempt to storm, but the inmates of the house and the fort were at their posts, and the loud and ringing voice of one of the women, Betsy Wheat—was heard about the din of the conflict urging the men to heroic deeds and cheering and encouraging them under the pressure of fatigue and exhaustion.

The attack proved abortive, and sullenly and slowly the Indians withdrew their forces nor did they attempt to storm again.

On the morning of the third day (13th), abandoning all hope of affecting their designs, they resolved on raising the siege. This resolution was announced to the inmates of the house and fort by a series of terrific yells and deafening whoops which gave expression to their disgust at the defeat which they had met. Turning their backs upon the fort, they took their departure and crossed the river in the neighborhood of what was formerly known as Beymer's landing, except a party of about one hundred warriors, who remained on the Virginia side of the river for the purpose of plundering and laying waste the settlements and the country in the vicinity of Western Virginia and Pennsylvania. On leaving, they drove away all the stock and carried off the portable property of the settlers and cut down and destroyed their crops.

During the siege their loss must have been serious, as the men who manned the house and fort were not in the habit of throwing away their shots but always tried to make each one effective. During the siege the whites lost none, and but one was wounded and he slightly. The persistence and courage displayed by the men and women both in the house and fort on this occasion was simply grand heroic.

We are able to give the names of many of those who were in the fort on this occasion and whose memories as well as names are worthy of perpetuation to the last syllable of recorded time. They are Silas Zane, who was in command, his brother, Andrew and Jonathan, Daniel Sullivan, Jacob Reikart and his brother George, James Smith and his two sons Henry and Thomas, Conrad Stoop, John Tait, Samuel Mills, Edward Mills, Thomas Mills, Hamilton Kerr, Alexander McDowell, Henry Clark, James Saltar, James Clark, Caspar French, Conrad Wheat and four sons, James Boggs, Martin and George Kerr, Peter Neiswanger, — Wright and the two men who accompanied Daniel Sullivan.

Of the women there were Lydia Boggs, Elizabeth Zane, Betsy Wheat and Miss Mary —, subsequently Mrs. Mary Burkitt.

During the siege two white men, who had been taken prisoners many years before by the Indians, and who had commands in their forces, deserted from them. They were arrested and taken prisoners by Colonel Swearingen, who with a force of a hundred men, was marching to the relief of the fort. From these men he learned of the intention of the Indians to abandon the siege on the morning following their desertion, and that their purpose was to detach a portion of their forces to operate in the adjacent country. He at once dispatched runners to convey the intelligence to the settlers in the surrounding country, and thus warned them of the meditated attack.

Betty Zane's run; from *Stories of American Life and Adventure* (1895)

During a portion of the siege, Elizabeth Zane, in company with her brother and a man named John Salter, occupied one of the bastions, and was engaged in loading their guns for them. The position was one of exposure and great danger. In after years she would tell her children and grandchildren how the whistling bullets in their deadly flight would knock the splinters from the roof and sides and cause them to fly so thick and fast that she was compelled to stop frequently and to pick them out of her hands, arms and the exposed portions of her person.

A Virginia frontier fort, similar to Fort Henry; from *History of the Early Settlement and Indian Wars of Western Virginia: Embracing an Account of the Various Expeditions in the West, Previous to 1795* (1851).

Not alone Elizabeth Zane, but every woman in the fort on this occasion proved herself a heroine. If some of them were less conspicuous, they were not less faithful, brave and true in their respective places.

Betsey Wheat, a woman of herculean strength and indomitable force of character, could with equal ability bear the butt end of a log, or use a rifle with the skill of a practiced woodsman. During the attack she would frequently relieve one of the sterner sex when exhausted, that he might obtain a brief respite and rest from fatigue and labor. Her stern voice urged the haggard to duty and cheered the heart and encouraged the spirits of the defenders. She recklessly exposed herself where danger was most imminent, fearless of consequences in the most defiant manner. In every emergency she was ready with expedients, and the greater the exigency, the more prompt was she to meet it.

Another worthy female requiring mention was Lydia Boggs, the daughter of Captain Boggs, then in the buoyancy of youth, and just entering the vestibule of young womanhood. Full of energy and fond of adventure, her woman's nature was crowned with a fortitude which neither knew nor feared danger. She hesitated not in the discharge of any duty, and quailed not before any difficulty, but her determined spirit and firm resolve enabled her to overcome every obstacle. She was unlike Betsey Wheat, in that she was less demonstrative in character, but not one whit less brave and faithful. Her ready hand moulded many a bullet during the siege, which became a missive of death to the besiegers, and loaded many a rifle which sounded the death knell of a foeman. But time would not permit us to individualize each heroine, did we possess the data which would enable us to do so. But suffice it to say that on this memorable occasion the women, with their moral force and material aid, made of success a triumph which their invincible spirits crowned with the unfading chaptlet of victory.[4]

****

Although from a national perspective the Second Battle of Fort Henry seems to be little-remembered, that's not the

---

[4] *The Sunday Register*, Wheeling, West Virginia, September 17, 1882.

case in Wheeling, West Virginia. The city not only abounds with historical markers calling attention to the fort, the battle, and its participants, but also stages a reenactment of the event from time-to-time, with authentically-costumed historical reenactors taking the place of the original participants. Video clips of these activities as well as a short professionally-made reenactment of Betty Zane's famous run for gunpowder can be viewed on YouTube.

If you leave Wheeling and travel about four miles upriver, to Walnut Grove Cemetery in Martin's Ferry, Ohio, where Betty Zane is buried, you'll find a statue of her on a pedestal, with a bronze plaque that reads: "In memory of Elizabeth Zane whose heroic deed saved Fort Henry in 1782."

Upon your return to downtown Wheeling, you can toast the memory of Betty, her brother Ebenezer, my 6th great-granduncle, Conrad Wheat, Jr., and all the other brave pioneers with a glass of Betsy Wheat I.P.A. (India Pale Ale) that's made by the Wheeling Brewing Company.

Finally, if or when someone ever asks you to name the last battle of the American Revolution, you can tell them the right answer, which isn't "Yorktown," and if they don't believe you, show them this story, or better yet, *buy them a copy of this book!*

FORREST LEADING HIS ROUGH RIDERS.

During the Civil War, Dan Seay was a cavalryman among the troops led by Gen. Nathan Bedford Forrest; from *Columbus and Columbia* (1893).

A Daring Escape

Of all the wars in which American soldiers have fought, our own Civil War is surely one of the most thoroughly covered in a typical U.S. History class. However, as I pointed out in this book's introduction, teachers don't have time to cover everything. Two topics that are often barely mentioned, if at all, are the activities of the U.S. and Confederate armies in the West, with the notable exception of the Siege of Vicksburg, where Confederate forces surrendered to Gen. Ulysses S. Grant on July 4, 1863, following a month-long siege, and Prisoner-of-War camps, except, perhaps, the infamous Andersonville stockade in Georgia, where Union P.O.W.s died by the scores from maltreatment.

I must admit that I was not particularly well-informed on either of these two subjects myself, that is until I discovered that I had a direct ancestor—my 2nd Great-Grandfather, Daniel P. Seay—who not only fought in the Western Tennessee campaign as a Confederate cavalryman under the command of the notorious Gen. Nathan Bedford Forrest, but also was captured and locked up in one of the most formidable Union P.O.W. facilities in the entire United States—a former fortress called Fort Delaware—*and then he escaped!* Or so the story goes. But did he really? Let's take a look.

****

Daniel Pitser Seay was the oldest son of Matthew A. and Elizabeth Ann (Lewis) Seay. He was born on November 30, 1845 or possibly 1847. His place of birth is also uncertain. In later life, Daniel himself claimed to have been born in Itawamba County, Mississippi, yet both he and his parents were listed as residents of McNairy County, Tennessee in the 1850 federal census, the first one following his birth. Moreover, all subsequent census records, from 1860 to and including 1880, give Tennessee as the state of his nativity. If he actually was born in Mississippi, it may have been while his mother was there visiting relatives or perhaps during a brief period of residency by his entire family.

According to family lore, soon after the Civil War began, when Union troops began military operations in Tennessee, "the Federals came" to the Seay family farm "and tore up the house & a book Daniel…had won at school." Afterward, it's been said, Dan vowed to "kill as many Yankees as there were pages in his book." It's also been alleged that another time "he drove [an] ox-team to town [where the] feds got [his] flour and meal." When this happened, "He went back [home] [to get [a] knife." Unfortunately, the teller of this story, one of Dan's sons, failed to say whether or not his father used it.

A Daring Escape

On July 1, 1863, when Dan Seay was not quite fifteen years old, if 1847 is the correct year of his birth, or nearly seventeen if born in 1845, using his middle name, Pitser, he was enlisted by Capt. W. T. Kizer at Jackson, Madison County, Tennessee, for service in the Confederate army as a private in Company E, 16th Tennessee Cavalry, Bell's Brigade, Buford's Division (a.k.a. Wilson's 21st Tennessee Cavalry), one of several units under the command of the controversial Gen. Nathan Bedford Forrest, future founder of the Ku Klux Klan. Dan's service record for March and April 1864 shows him "present" for duty.

Although Dan's time in service was relatively short—less than two years—and the details hard to come by—from all appearances it was eventful. Family lore holds that on one occasion, at a crossroads near Memphis, when surrounded by federal soldiers, Dan and three other men escaped by riding their horses through enemy lines, with only "one man hurt."[1]

It's said that another time, Dan and his comrades captured a Union officer, together with his "horse & his gun," and personally delivered their prisoner to Gen. Nathan Bedford Forrest, which made him feel "as big as the Gen. himself."[2]

---

[1] Recollections of Mark M. Seay, son of Daniel P. Seay, interviewed by Joyce Calcote Drew and Maude Seay Prince, date unknown, but sometime prior to 1971;
[2] Ibid.

Family lore holds further that Dan had a "spirited horse" that "carried him into enemy lines," which, unfortunately for him, resulted in his capture. Precisely when and where this happened has apparently been lost to history, but it's been said that afterward, he was taken to and "held in [Fort] Delaware Prison,"[3] on Pea Patch Island, which was (and still is) located in the middle of the Delaware River, about fifty miles below Philadelphia. Star-shaped, with thick walls made of gray stone, the fort was first built after British successes in the War of 1812 awakened the U.S. government to the fact that with only a few exceptions, such as Baltimore, the nation's ports and large cities were woefully unprotected against the possibility of foreign invasion. The present edifice, which is the same one in which Dan Seay was allegedly incarcerated, was built in 1859 to replace an earlier fort of the same name.

What was life like for rebel prisoners at Fort Delaware? Unfortunately, we have nothing from Dan in his own words, but the following information, provided to a Southern newspaper by a P.O.W., paints a grim picture of the place:

> At the time of his leaving Fort Delaware some two weeks ago, it was estimated that there were confined there about 8000 prisoners. This large number, with the exception of about 1000, taken in the battle of Champion Hill, are all prisoners taken from General Lee's army, principally at the battle of Gettysburg and in his campaign in Maryland and Pennsylvania.

---

[3] Ibid.

A Daring Escape

Fort Delaware, where Daniel P. Seay was allegedly held as a prisoner-of-war during the Civil War. U.S. Government photo.

The treatment of our prisoners beggars all description. Fort Delaware is said to present within its walls all the horrors of the Hole of Calcutta. The sufferings of our men was so great, and the treating so extremely cruel, that disease had broken out among them, and was sweeping them off by hundreds. The hospitals were crowded, and the mortality, our informant thinks, could not be less than twenty-five a day. Yet this did not seem enough to assuage the malignity and vindictiveness of the Yankees, and so far from exciting their pity, it secured but to incite them to fresh deeds of inhumanity. The way our dead are buried at Fort Delaware tells of itself in the devilish spirit that reigns there. They are taken out to the government farm on the Jersey coast, near by the fort, and shoved, not buried, under the ground, in a hole dug six feet by six.

The disease that is committing fearful ravages among our prisoners at Fort Delaware is a dysentery, of a malignant type, superinduced by the dirty, miserable water, and the half-putrefied meat that is dealt out to one. It is no exaggeration to say the accounts we get of the fate of our men in Fort Delaware exceed anything we have heard of during the war. The quantity of bread allowed to each man is but six crackers a day! The meat is the toughest, poorest kind of beef, such as is bought up the shoddy [word uncertain], and is often so offensive, from the warm weather, that it cannot be brought within six inches of the mouth. Worse than all, the water used is nothing but the pumpings from the bay, and when the wind blows from the sea, it is made so bad that it is but little better than the runnings of a sewer. The fare of our men is so bad that it is a practice of the prison to offer, as an inducement, three meals of soft bread and a bit of tobacco, to any of our men who will assist in the work and drudgery of the prison and yard. So great had become the torture of life in Fort Delaware that some of our men, rather than endure it longer, had taken the oath of allegiance, and been set at liberty, though without a friend or dollar in the world. Our informant, who is a South Carolinian himself, tells us that he saw a man from his own State, who owned slaves, and of whose fealty and devotion to our cause there could be no doubt, take the oath of allegiance rather than "die by inches," as he expressed it, "in Fort Delaware."[4]

Another Confederate soldier, who had been captured at the Battle of Gettysburg, told of how he and his comrade were brought to the fort on a boat that transited the Delaware Canal, of his arrival there, and how the prisoners were housed:

> I was wet when I got on the [canal] boat, but the firemen allowed me to stand around the boilers, and when we reached

---

[4] *Richmond Examiner*, Richmond, Virginia, August 21, 1863.

Delaware City, at the end of the canal, and opposite Fort Delaware, my clothing was about dry. We were carried over to the fort without delay, and were put in some wooden buildings, which had three tiers of bunks on either side. The barracks were of Northern pine, and the planks were nailed on up and down. The roofs were covered with tarred paper. There were some windows in openings.

These were long buildings about 20 feet wide, and were built so as to inclose a square. On the inside of the square was the yard. All of the openings in the building were on the inside. The openings in the building which communicated with the outside, was on the side next to the fort. Part of these buildings was used as a kitchen and dining hall. The sink was on the levee on the north side of the island, and was built so as to extend out over the water in the river. The buildings were on the north side of the island, so situated that they were exposed to a broadside of the fort, the huge columbiads of which were kept constantly trained on the prisoners. The fort was garrisoned by some Regulars of heavy artillery, while the infantry garrison, at first, consisted of a regiment of Delaware troops.

The island was about a mile from the Delaware shore, and about a mile and a quarter from the Jersey shore. The surface of the island was below the level of the waters of the river and was protected from overflow by a levee of earth and stone. Canals extend over the island, and were filled with brackish water, which kept them from getting too stagnant, as would have been the case had the waters in them been fresh, since there was no way to have a constant inflow and outflow.

The fort was casemated, and was situated on the Jersey side of the island. There were two wharves, one opposite Delaware City, and the other on the opposite side, near the fort.

Within a few days after I arrived the Confederate soldiers confined there numbered more than 10,000, there being more from North Carolina than any other State.

The guards were stationed inside and outside of the pen, and some were posted on the levee. There was no hospital on the island for some time, and the doctors came inside the pen and treated the sick and wounded on their bunks. The majority of the Confederates were from the field of Gettysburg, and every Southern State was represented.[5]

Unsurprisingly, some prisoners attempted to escape. Unlucky ones were shot while trying. In 1863, a Southern newspaper reported how one group managed to get away:

> Yesterday afternoon five Confederate prisoners…arrived here from Fort Delaware, having made their escape from Fort Delaware on the night of the 12th inst. The narrative of their escape is interesting. Having formed the plan of escape, they improvised life preservers by tying four canteens, well-corked, around the body of each man, and on the night of the 12th inst. proceeded to leave the island. The night being dark, they got into the water and swam off from the back of the island for the shore. Three of them swam four miles, and landed about two miles below Delaware City; the other two, being swept down the river, floated down sixteen miles, and landed at Christine Creek. Another soldier (a Philadelphian) started with them, but was drowned a short distance from the shore. He said he was not coming back to the Confederacy, but was going to Philadelphia. He had eight canteens around his body, but was not an expert swimmer.
>
> The three who landed near Delaware City laid in a cornfield all night, and the next evening, about dark, started on their way South, after first having made known their condition to a farmer, who gave them a good supper. They traveled that night 12 miles through Kent County, Delaware, and the next day lay concealed in a gentleman's barn. From there they went to Kent County, Md., where the citizens gave them new clothes and money. After this their detection was less probable, as they had been

---

[5] *The National Tribune*, Washington, D.C., April 17, 1902.

wearing their uniforms the two days previous. They took the cars on the Philadelphia and Baltimore Railroad to Dover, the capital of Delaware. Sitting near them in the cars were a Yankee Colonel and Captain, and the provost guard passed through frequently. They were not discovered, however, though to escape detection seemed almost impossible. They got off the train at Delamar and went by way of Barren Creek Springs and Quantico, Md., to the Nanticoke river, and got into a canoe.

Here they parted, in company with five others who had escaped from Fort Delaware some days previous, as the canoe would not hold ten of them. In the canoe they went to Tangier's Sound, and crossing below the Chesapeake, landed in Northumberland county, below Point Lookout, a point at which the Yankees are building a fort for the confinement of prisoners. They met with great kindness from citizens of Heathsville, who contributed $120 to aid them on their route. They soon met with our pickets, and came to this city on York River Railroad. These escaped prisoners express in the liveliest terms their gratitude to the people of Maryland and Delaware [two slave states that did not secede], who did everything they could to aid them. There was no difficulty experienced in either State in finding generous people of Southern sympathies, who would give them both money and clothing, and put themselves to any trouble to help them on their journey.

These gentlemen state that a large number of our prisoners at Fort Delaware have taken the oath and enlisted in the Yankee service. The Yankees have already, from prisoners who have taken the oath, enlisted 270 men in the 3rd Maryland cavalry, 160 men in a battalion of heavy artillery, and 150 in an infantry regiment. To effect these enlistments they circulated all sorts of lies among the prisoners. The chief lies are to the effect that Gen. Lee has resigned—that North Carolina has withdrawn from the Confederacy and sent commissioners from the State on to Washington to make terms for re-entering the Union, and that Virginia is only waiting for Lee's army to be driven from her borders to resume her connection with the Yankee nation.

They tell the men, if they will enlist, they will be sent out West to fight the Indians, and will never be sent South, where there would be any danger of their capture. When a prisoner agrees to enlist, his name is put down in a book, and he is marched from the main body of the prisoners to another part of the island to join his companions in shame, who live in tents there. He never comes back among his old comrades, for fear, as one of our informants remarked, "we should cut his d—d throat." They are jeered and hooted by their late companions as they pass out from them. They are termed "galvanized Yankees."

Our prisoners are dying at Fort Delaware at the rate of twelve a day. Their rations are six crackers a day and spoilt beef.[6]

According to his son, Mark M. Seay, Dan escaped from Fort Delaware with a prisoner named Wilson (whether first name or last name is unknown)—and others perhaps—by lifting up some floorboards in the building in which they were housed. (If this is true, then it means that they were housed in the wooden barracks that lay outside the prison proper.) Then, with his clothes on his head, he "swam 7 miles to the other side" of the Delaware River. The distance from Pea Patch Island to the Delaware mainland is only about a mile-and-a-half. If Dan went as far as seven miles, he must have been carried downstream by the current, which is not only possible but likely. The Delaware is a big, fast flowing river. After reaching shore, he "saw [a] big house and went to [the] back door & asked for food." The

---

[6] *Richmond Dispatch*, Richmond, Virginia, August 25, 1863.

man who answered told him to hide in a nearby plum thicket and he would bring him food. After what seemed like a long time, the man "came with [a] basket of fried chicken & biscuits & they ate until their tongues got tired."[7]

Unfortunately, the truth of this story cannot be ascertained because Dan Seay's name isn't found on any extant prison roster of Fort Delaware and his service record makes no mention of his alleged captivity either. Neither was his capture or escape reported in the press. In short, there is no corroborating evidence. One expert has opined that in the absence of any proof, the story almost certainly isn't true, conjecturing that when Dan Seay told his children about his service in the Civil War, he may have taken other veterans' stories that he'd heard and made them his own. Ordinarily, I would concur with that assessment because that's very possible. However, I do not think that the absence of Dan Seay's name on a P.O.W. roster means that his incarceration and escape is a complete fabrication. The Fort Delaware Society, which maintains a database of Confederate P.O.W.s and responds to queries (a service I've utilized), states that if one's ancestor cannot be found in the available records that doesn't necessarily mean the soldier wasn't there. Why? Because as the Society admits, some of the records are "sketchy" and others are missing altogether.

---

[7] Recollections of Mark M. Seay, son of Daniel P. Seay, interviewed by Joyce Calcote Drew and Maude Seay Prince, date unknown, but sometime prior to 1971; transcribed in a letter sent to Inez Jenkins Hickman by Mrs. Drew, probably 1977.

Something else that should be taken into consideration is the fact that people can, and do, "fall through the cracks," so to speak, when it comes to official records. Here's an example from my own life: When I was in the Navy, I went on two long cruises aboard two different aircraft carriers. At the conclusion of each of those deployments, I received an official U.S. Navy cruise book (something like a high school or college annual). Inside was a photo of every man who was aboard ship during the cruise, identified by name, rank and department or squadron. In the first of these cruise books, there I am, for everyone to see. So clearly, I was aboard. However, if you examine the second cruise book from cover-to-cover, you would have to conclude that I didn't go on that cruise. Why? Because my name and photo are nowhere to be seen. Why not? Because when the photos for my squadron were taken, I was temporarily assigned to the ship's Master-at-Arms force, and by the time the ship's photographer had got around to taking a group photo of the Master-at-Arms force, I had returned to my squadron. So, even though I was aboard the ship the entire six months, no one looking at the cruise book would think so.

What I am trying to say is that although I cannot tell you that Dan Seay's escape from Fort Delaware definitely happened the way his son said it did, it's not out of the realm of possibility. We do know that Dan Seay was in the Confederate Army in 1863 and 1864, when Fort Delaware was being used to incarcerate Confederate P.O.W.s.

Furthermore, Dan's son did not just say that his father was a prisoner, he specified Fort Delaware as the place of incarceration and described the sort of escape that required crossing a river, and furthermore, the story he told was similar to descriptions of other escapes. Unfortunately, the story is incomplete. Mark Seay said nothing about what happened after his father was fed a meal of fried chicken and biscuits in a plum orchard near the banks of the Delaware River. As a descendant of Dan Seay, I'd like the story to be true. If it is, it's likely that his return South was similar to the experience of the five men whose escape from the fort is described earlier in this chapter.

There's something else that's occurred to me. According to Dan's service record, he deserted on June 22, 1864 at Tupelo, Mississippi. I think this could be a mistake and that instead, it may have been the day his "spirited" horse carried him through Union lines, where he was captured. Anyone on the Confederate side seeing him galloping toward Union lines might have erroneously concluded that he was going over to the enemy, but clearly that was not the case if he was sent to Fort Delaware.

My theory is supported by the fact that federal troops commanded by Gen. Andrew Jackson Smith marched from Moscow, Tennessee into Mississippi on June 22, 1864, in order to keep General Forrest's cavalry, numbering about 6,000 men, distracted while troops under the command of Union General William Tecumseh Sherman were busy advancing on Atlanta, Georgia. This is the same date that Dan Seay's service record says he deserted and of course, he was one of Forrest's soldiers. I should reiterate, however, that this theory that his capture was mistaken for desertion is entirely conjecture on my part, *but it's not unlikely.*

There's one more thing to consider: Some years after Dan Seay moved to Texas, he applied to the State of Texas for a Confederate pension. One of the witnesses to his character and the veracity of the statements he made on the application was a man named John T. Rodgers, who stated under oath that he had known Dan Seay in Tennessee and that they had served together in the same company of the same regiment throughout the war. When Rodgers applied for a pension, Dan Seay did the same for him. Unfortunately, neither mentioned captivity, but there is a roster of Confederate P.O.W.s at Fort Delaware that bears the name of John T. Rodgers, who was there until war's end, when he was paroled. Was this Dan's friend, who for some reason did not himself escape from the fortress? Could be.

There's one more possibility and that's that Mark Seay misremembered, and therefore he might have been mistaken about which P.O.W. facility Dan escaped from. Unfortunately, I have not had time to examine all the rosters of all thirty-four prisons or camps the Union operated during the Civil War.

But one thing is certain. I am much better informed on this subject than previously, *and now, so are you!*

A Blessing in Disguise

Dan Seay was not the only one of my ancestors taken prisoner during the Civil War (see chapter entitled "A Daring Escape"). Another, who also served as a soldier from the South, was likewise captured, only instead of escaping like Dan allegedly did, he waited patiently until a prisoner exchange could be arranged, at which time he rejoined his regiment and resumed his military service. As it turned out, getting taken prisoner was probably one of the best things that ever happened to him. Why? Because while he was locked up under Federal guard, his regiment took part in not just one, but *three* bloody battles, where, if he had been present, he might very well have been killed. Thus, what must have seemed to him at the time as an unfortunate turn-of-events, was actually a blessing in disguise—a "lucky break" I like to call it—that greatly increased his chances of surviving the war, which he did. Now, here is his story:

****

In February 1861, despite the outspoken opposition of Governor Sam Houston—who was forced out of office when he refused to take an oath of allegiance to the

Confederacy—the State of Texas seceded from the Union and joined the newly formed Confederate States of America. On April 15, 1861, the Civil War officially began when President Lincoln declared the southern states in rebellion after South Carolina troops fired on Fort Sumter in Charleston harbor. A little more than a year later and only a month or so short of his sixteenth birthday, my 2nd Great-Grandfather, Morris Ward Jr., enlisted as a private in Company D, 28th Texas Cavalry (Dismounted). The date was May 9, 1862. His term of service was three years or the duration of the war. There is some uncertainty as to the place of his enlistment. One card in his service record file reads Upshur County, which was his home county. Another says Wood County, which is immediately adjacent to Upshur. A third says he enlisted at Starrville, which is in Smith County, immediately to the south of both Wood and Upshur.[1] All three are located in the heart of the piney woods of East Texas, so I guess it doesn't matter much. Either way, he was in the Confederate Army! He also served briefly, by order of his commanding officer, in the 4th Texas Light Artillery, Captain Horace Halderman (or Haldeman), commanding, which was a part of the same division (Walker's) as the 28th Texas Cavalry. This was from May to about November 1863.

---

[1] Civil War Service Records, Confederate, Morris Ward, Jr., National Archives, Washington, D.C.

Interestingly, like three-fourths of all white Southerners, Morris Ward, Jr. did not come from a slave-holding family. According to the 1860 federal census his father, a simple yeoman farmer, owned a measly $150 worth of personal property. (The value of his real estate was left unrecorded.) Although it is an indisputable fact that the southern states were led into secession by a relatively small group of powerful slaveholding politicians, in order to protect and perpetuate the institution of African slavery, it is doubtful that my then-young ancestor gave much thought to such matters. At fifteen, an age at which few individuals are capable of critical thinking, especially in a state where even the rudiments of an education were hard to come by, he was almost certainly told, and probably believed in all sincerity, that by joining up he would be defending "his country" against Northern invaders who wanted to destroy Southern "rights,"-which at that time included the dubious right to hold human beings in bondage against their will.

Because young Ward left no journal or letters that we know of, his personal experiences of the war are unknowable. Fortunately, the movements of his regiment and the battles in which they participated have been well documented.

The leader of the 28th Texas Cavalry was Colonel Horace Randal, a West Point graduate and former U.S. army officer. When the Civil War began, Randal resigned his U.S. Army commission. Almost immediately, the Confederate government offered him a commission as a second lieutenant, but he refused it. Instead, he fought as a private soldier in Virginia before returning to Texas. In 1862, he became an officer once again.

During the summer of 1862, after Randal took over as colonel of the 28th Texas Cavalry, the regiment became part of the 2nd Brigade of General John G. Walker's Texas Division. It had previously been brigaded under General Ben McCulloch of Texas Ranger fame. This division was the largest unit of Texans in the war. These troops, by their frequent long marches over the too-often muddy roads of Arkansas and Louisiana, soon earned the nickname "Walker's Greyhounds."

The first battle in which the 28th Texas Cavalry participated was at Milliken's Bend (June 7, 1863), which occurred during the Vicksburg campaign (spring and summer 1863). They later took part in the Battle of Mansfield (April 8, 1864), and the Battle of Pleasant Hill (April 9, 1864). At the latter, Colonel Randal was fatally wounded. As it happened, Private Ward was involved in only one of these three contests (Milliken's Bend), which may be why he survived the war when so many others, including the colonel of his regiment, did not.

The battles of Mansfield and Pleasant Hill occurred as a result of a Union campaign, in the spring of 1864, to capture Shreveport, Louisiana, and then, if that went well, to invade Texas from the east, and ultimately, to occupy it. Once the

Confederates learned of this offensive, Walker's division sprang into action, leaving the vicinity of Marksville, Louisiana, where they'd been camped for some time, and moving to the vicinity of Cheneyville. Of course, these troops included the 28th Texas Cavalry (Dismounted). It was around this same time that Private Ward and thirty-three of his fellow soldiers from Company D were reassigned to help defend Fort DeRussy, a Confederate stronghold that lay on the Red River, near its confluence with the Mississippi. Upon arrival at the fort, or shortly thereafter, Morris and his comrades were given the job of manning the fort's water battery beside the Red River, located about 700 yards east of the main fortification.

Here's a description of Fort Derussy, nicknamed the "Confederate Gibraltar," which appeared in a Nashville, Tennessee newspaper:

> Fort Derussy is a most formidable work, quadrangular shaped, and bastions and bombproofs covered with railroad iron. A powerful water battery [the one to which Private Ward was assigned] connects with the fort, the casements of which are capable of resisting shot and shell of the heaviest calibre. The position of the guns [is] capital for rapid and effective fire on all boats attempting to go up or down the river. About 600 negro men were employed for one year constructing this fort.[2]

---

[2] *The Nashville Daily Union*, Nashville, Tennessee, March 26, 1864.

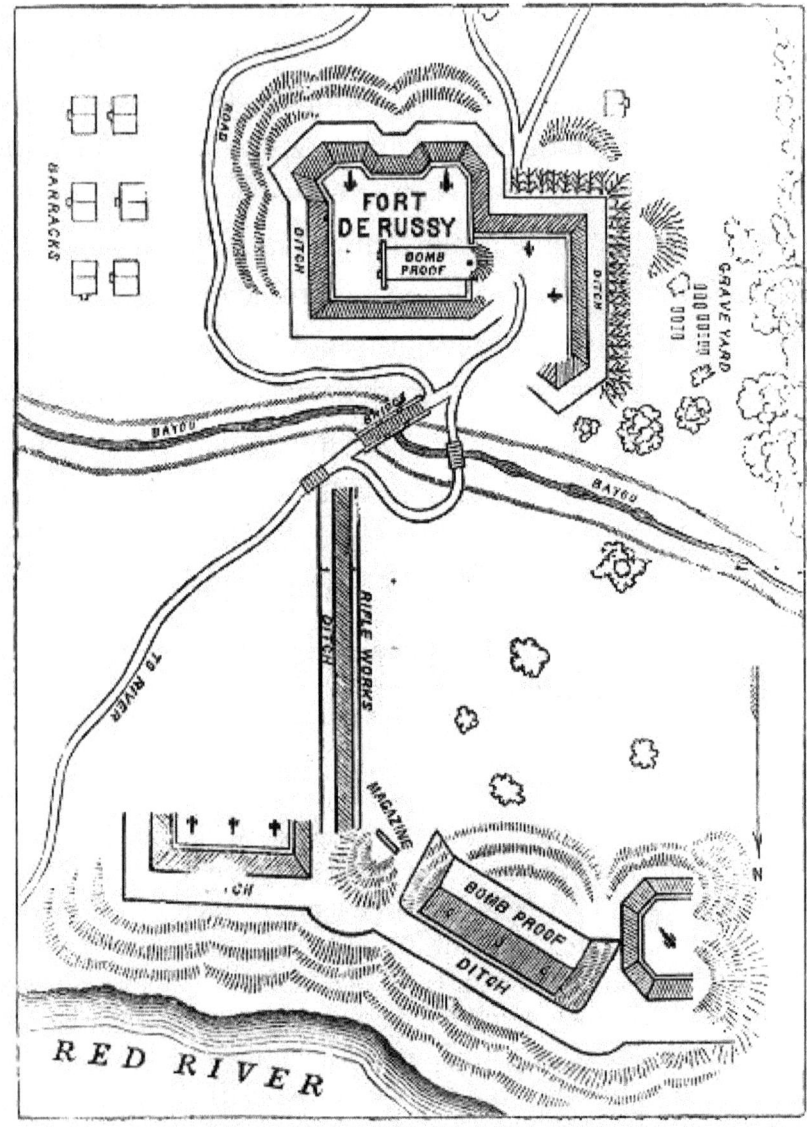

Plan of Fort DeRussy. The battery that Morris War helped to defend is on the left, near the river; from *Harper's Weekly*, vol. 8, April 30, 1864, p. 277.

As it happened, Fort Derussy was not as Gibraltar-like as it had been made out to be. On March 14, 1864, after being pounded by artillery from Union gunboats in the Red River and attacked landside by Union troops for only a short time, the 350-man garrison of the supposedly impregnable fortress quickly surrendered. Although several men managed to escape into the woods and rejoin their regiment, young Morris Ward, Jr. was among the twelve men from the 28th who were taken prisoner by the Federals. In a report composed in 1865, a Union General, A. J. Smith, recalled the attack, and ultimately the surrender, of Fort DeRussy:

"Capture of Fort DeRussy"; from *Frank Leslie's Illustrated Newspaper,* April 9, 1864, p. 41.

On arriving near the fort I found that it was occupied by a garrison of about 350 men. I therefore halted my column 1½ miles from the fort, and, after covering my left flank and rear from any attack that Walker could possibly make, directed General Mower to advance with the First and Second Brigades of the Third Division, Sixteenth Army Corps, in line of battle, with skirmishers thrown well to the front, followed by the Third Brigade within supporting distance. As soon as the line came within sight of the fort the enemy opened upon it with five pieces of artillery from the fort, doing, however, but little execution. Their guns on the land side all being en barbette, the skirmishers of the Second Brigade soon silenced them. At about 6:30 p.m. the order to charge was given, and the First and Second Brigades advanced under a scattering fire from the enemy, whose infantry were kept down by my skirmishers, and scaled the parapet within twenty minutes from the time the order to charge was given. The enemy then surrendered. Our loss was 3 killed and 35 wounded; total 38. Full lists of casualties and captures accompany this report. We captured 319 prisoners, 10 pieces of artillery, and a large quantity of ordnance and ordnance stores. Among the pieces of artillery taken were two 9-inch Dahlgren guns.[3]

Following the fall of Fort DeRussy, Pvt. Morris Ward and his fellow P.O.W.s were taken on gunboats to Baton Rouge, where they were kept in the state penitentiary for three days. On the evening of March 17, they again boarded boats—only this time they were taken to New Orleans, where they arrived on March 18.

New Orleans had been captured by Union forces under General Benjamin Butler and Admiral David Farragut in

---

[3] *War of the Rebellion: A Compilation of the Official Records of the Union and Confederate Armies, Series I, Vol. XXXIV, Part 1-Reports* (Washington, D.C.: Government Printing Office, 1891), 305.

April 1862. Prior to that time, Union P.O.W.s had been incarcerated at New Orleans. From thereon, the shoe was on the other foot. Now, captured Confederates filled the cells.

New Orleans Parish Prison, where Morris Ward, Jr. may have been incarcerated following his capture at Fort Derussy; from *Harper's Weekly*, Vol. XXXIV, No. 1768, November 1890.

Although official records do not show the name of the facility where Morris Ward was incarcerated during his nearly four-month-long captivity, in all likelihood it would have been at one of three places. One was the New Orleans Parish Prison, a three-story-tall stone structure built in 1834 and bounded by Orleans, St. Ann, Treme, and Marais streets-near where the Mahalia Jackson Auditorium and

Louis Armstrong Park are located today. The prison was demolished in 1894 and replaced with a more modern structure, which has also since been torn down.

The Customs House is another possibility. Built in 1848, it is still standing today at 423 Canal Street. Reportedly, it housed as many as 2,000 prisoners at one time.

Rebel prisoners in the New Orleans Custom House; from *Harper's Weekly*, August 29, 1863. Was Private Morris Ward kept here?

The so-called "Cotton Press Prison," more properly Picayune Cotton Press No. 4, located on the levee in the

First District, at the corner of Levee and Montegut streets, was also used to incarcerate Confederate P.O.W.s. The Union Cotton Press on Terpsichore Street is said to have been likewise utilized for that purpose. From all accounts, these warehouse-like structures where during peacetime ginned cotton was pressed into large bales, were reportedly cleaner and more comfortable than most Civil War prisons, although when overcrowded, they could be, and often were, conducive to the spread of sickness. Upon arrival at the "Cotton Press Prison," one rebel, clearly in good spirits, wrote to a friend back home:

> How do you like the name of our magnificent-and most secluded-quiet & safe Hotel? Ha ha—Cotton Press Prison!! In olden times these places used to be for the accommodation of Cotton but now it is for our especial benefit [sic]—Our Rebs!! Perhaps-they think we are Cotton [sic] or something of the kind. Wonder what kind of linen and cotton cloth we would make-if we were shipped North…We are in here about 850. Our quarters are pretty good-but too much crowded. There is also a good deal of sickness—As many as 5 and six cases of Small-pox go to the hospital every day. Young Lejuene…is down with it & at the hospital—he belongs to the 2d. La Cav. Nuka Longuepu is also in the hospital-suffering with Rheumatism & Fevers. Emile Broussard, Charley Bergeron & one of Charley's brothers are also in here. They have all been quite sick but are now well and getting along pretty well.[4]

---

[4] Letter from Frank Babin to Miss Henrietta Lauzin, May 14, 1864, Cotton Press Prison, New Orleans, Louisiana [Louisiana Digital Library, [https://louisianadigitallibrary.org/islandora/search/mods_subject_topic_ms:%22Prisoners%5C%20and%5C%20prisons%22; accessed 8 April 2021].

Federal records state that Ward rejoined his regiment on July 22, 1864 at "Red River, Louisiana," when Union and Confederate prisoners were exchanged.[5] Of course, there is no way to know his state of mind, but we may suppose he was relieved, but perhaps at the same time upset by having missed so much action. No doubt he and his fellow P.O.W.s were the butt of much good-natured "hurrahing" by their battle-hardened comrades. At that time, the 28th Texas Cavalry (Dismounted) was stationed about 20 miles southwest of Alexandria. The following day, they broke camp, marching to Harrisonburg, where the regiment remained until August 26.

Here's what I think is most important about my ancestor's captivity: Because of it, Private Ward missed the Battle of Mansfield (April 8, 1864) and also the Battle of Pleasant Hill, Louisiana (April 9, 1864), as well as the Battle of Jenkins' Ferry, Arkansas (April 30, 1864), where the 28th Texas Cavalry (Dismounted) suffered their heaviest casualties of the war: 38 killed, 95 wounded (many severely), and 2 missing. There is of course no way to know if he would have been among the dead or wounded had he been there, but it seems a fair bet to conclude that apart from the possible danger of contracting an illness, my 2nd Great-Grandfather was almost certainly safer as a P.O.W. in New Orleans. As I said at the beginning of this chapter, I see it as

---

[5], U.S. Civil War Prisoner of War Records, 1861-1865, Selected Records of the War Department Relating to Confederate Prisoners of War, 1861-1865, Roll of Prisoners of War, New Orleans, La., 393.

a blessing in disguise, a lucky break that kept him out of harm's way. I wonder: Did he see it that way too?

As it happened, the remainder of Private Ward's service was largely uneventful. Between August 1864 and May 1865, when the regiment finally disbanded, the men spent their time in a variety of camps located in Northern Louisiana and Southern Arkansas, where they drilled, held inspections, and performed mock battles for the entertainment of the local populace. When in the late spring of 1865 it became obvious that the war was lost, many men deserted. Finally, in mid-May, the entire brigade simply disbanded, and everyone went home.

****

At war's end, Morris Ward, Jr. returned to his home in East Texas, where in 1869 he married a young woman named Mary Ann Lowry, daughter of an older Confederate veteran, Mark Lowry of Starrville, and began having children, one of which was my great-grandmother Margaret or "Maggie" Ward, born in 1875.

From war's end to 1894, a period of nearly three decades, Morris Ward, Jr. and his family lived on a farm that lay on the north bank of the Sabine River, which was almost certainly left to him by his father. He enlarged it in 1878 with the purchase of an adjacent 200-acre tract. During this time, he also bought and operated a steam mill.

In 1880 Morris's wife died, shortly after giving birth to her fifth child. Unfortunately, the baby did not survive much longer.

In 1894, Morris' daughter, Maggie, married Dan Seay's oldest son, Matthew, and then went to live in Lamar County. Morris moved there too, settling near a rural community called Blossom. The following year, he married a widow named Molly Thompson, with whom he had another child. About this same time, Morris wrote to Dan Seay, the father of his son-in-law, urging Dan and his wife, Martha, to move up to Blossom too, *and they did*!

Although I have no way of knowing, I'd bet that during the short time they knew one another, Dan Seay and Morris Ward, Jr. were friends. Not only did they have grandchildren in common, but each had also served in the Confederate Army during the Civil War, and entirely by chance, both had been prisoners-of-war: Dan at Fort Delaware and Morris in New Orleans. In my mind's eye, I can imagine them sitting in rocking chairs on the front porch of a farmhouse, chewing tobacco, or smoking cigars, drinking whiskey, and swapping war stories. Unfortunately, the two men did not have a lot of time together. Morris Ward, Jr. died about 1903, only a few years after Dan Seay had moved to Lamar County, and was buried, most likely in the same little country cemetery—Red Oak—where Dan was laid to rest a quarter of a century later. So, dear reader, don't you agree that it's only fitting that these two men should also be included in this book?

Connections to Lincoln

Because he championed the abolition of slavery and also because he preserved the Union, Abraham Lincoln is almost universally ranked as the greatest American President. Only Franklin D. Roosevelt, who led this country through the Great Depression and World War II, comes nearest the number one spot.

As I pointed out in the Introduction to this book, because former President Barack Obama and I share a common ancestor on his mother's side, as well as on mine, he and I are distant cousins. As it happens, I can say the same thing about President Harry Truman (through the same common ancestor as Obama), and on my father's side, through a different ancestor—an early Virginia immigrant named Christopher Branch—Thomas Jefferson is likewise a distant cousin. Unfortunately, I can't say the same about Abraham Lincoln. I *am* pleased to say, however, that on my mother's side of the family, I can point with pride to no fewer than four ancestral connections to the "Great Emancipator."

****

The first of these "Lincoln Connections" involves an ancestor, Samuel Haycraft, Sr., who was among the founders of Hardin County, Kentucky, which is where Abraham Lincoln was born on February 12, 1809. If you have been reading this book in order, rather than haphazardly, you already know that Samuel Haycraft's Revolutionary War experiences are the subject of the chapter entitled "McIntosh's 'Stepping Stone.'"

As previously noted, while still serving in the Continental Army at Fort Pitt, in Western Pennsylvania, Samuel was married to a young woman named Margaret Van Meter. Shortly after his term of service expired, he and his bride joined her parents and several other families that traveled on rafts down the Ohio River to start a new life in a region then known as "Kaintuck."

Samuel Haycraft, Sr. was not only one of the founders of Elizabethtown, Kentucky, which is the seat of Hardin County, he also became one of the town's most prominent and prosperous citizens, and in 1796-'97 he decided to build a sawmill on Severns Valley Creek, southeast of Elizabethtown's courthouse square and just outside the town limits. To help him in this ambitious endeavor, Samuel hired a local man named Thomas Lincoln—yes, *that* Thomas Lincoln, none other than Abraham Lincoln's father.

Today, the tiny Haycraft Mill Patio Park, located on the east side of the East Dixie Highway, adjacent to the 1936 "Lincoln-Haycraft Memorial Bridge," commemorates the old mill. On the same side of the road, but opposite side of the bridge, a Kentucky state historical marker likewise calls attention to it. Both the bridge and a bronze historical plaque, embedded in the northwest capstone, were formally dedicated on November 6, 1936, at a ceremony attended by local, state, and federal officials, including a United States Senator.

It's possible that the Haycraft Mill resembled this old mill in nearby Bardstown Kentucky; courtesy Library of Congress.

The wording of the imbedded plaque, which can still be seen to this day, reads as follows:

> Here on Severns Valley Creek Samuel Haycraft Senior, in the year 1797, built a mill and race way. Thomas Lincoln, father

of the 16th president of the United States, was employed to assist in the construction of the primitive mill, and it was there that he received his first regular, monetary wages.

Abraham Lincoln in the year 1816, when but seven years of age, migrated with his family westward, crossing Severns Valley Creek to enter Elizabethtown, Kentucky, enroute to the State of Indiana.

According to Gerald McMurtry, an Elizabethtown native whose extensive research into the Lincoln family's Hardin County connections almost certainly remains unsurpassed, Samuel Haycraft, Sr.'s account books (which are reportedly incomplete) reveal that Lincoln was hired "to excavate ground for a mill race" and that Haycraft paid him "three shillings a day or four or five shillings a rod, depending on the condition of the soil," for a total of 39 shillings on his first pay day, July 13, 1796. In another article McMurtry states that Lincoln (who was then only twenty years old) was paid $9.56. Since I have not actually examined Haycraft's account books myself, I am uncertain which form of payment—shillings or dollars—is correct. I think we may safely assume, however, that the payments were in shillings and that the dollar amount stated was an attempt by McMurtry to convert the original entries into modern-day money for the benefit of his readers, who almost certainly would not know the value of a shilling circa 1796-1797. McMurtry goes on to say that Lincoln received a total of £24 for all his work. In one of the numerous articles that he penned for the *Hardin County Enterprise* (which were later reprinted).¹ Here is how the intrepid historian broke it down:

September 1, credited with six days work on mill dam. September 9, paid $48.65 by Haycraft. September 12, credited with six days work on mill dam. September 17, received $6.62 from Haycraft; October 1797, credited with three days' work on mill dam. December, credited with six days work on mill dam; Received on dates not given, $52.49; $33.09.²

We are also informed that around this same time, young Lincoln purportedly constructed a Cherry Wood Sugar Chest for Peggy Haycraft, Samuel Sr.'s wife.³

Kentucky State historical marker commemorating the Lincoln-Haycraft connection; author photo.

---

[1] Gerald McMurtry, A Series of Monographs Concerning the Lincolns and Hardin County, Kentucky (Elizabethtown, Kentucky: 1938), 126.
[2] Gerald McMurtry, "Highlights of the History of Hardin County: Lincoln and the Haycrafts," *Hardin County Enterprise,* Elizabethtown, Kentucky, August 26, 1936.
[3] "Furniture made by Thomas Lincoln," Lincoln Lore, Ft. Wayne Indiana, No. 1512, February 1964, 2-3.

Unfortunately, Samuel Haycraft's sawmill, which he sold in 1803 to Henry Ewing (in exchange for 125 acres of land), was demolished at some point in the distant past and historical references to it are hard to come by. There seem to be no pictures of it either, but in all likelihood, it looked something like a mill constructed in Bardstown, in neighboring Nelson County, which was still standing and photographed circa 1900 for a postcard (reproduced on page 145).

****

Our second Lincoln connection likewise involves Samuel Haycraft, Sr., only this time, it was the then-future President's then-future stepmother, Sarah ("Sally") Bush Johnston, widow of Daniel Johnston, who was the party of the second part.

On March 17, 1818, for $25, Samuel Haycraft, Sr. sold the future Mrs. Lincoln a one-and-one-quarter acre lot in Elizabethtown. The sale included the small cabin (14 x 14 feet) in which Johnston and her three children were then living.[4] According to all accounts, Thomas Lincoln, who resided in Hardin County from 1796 to 1816, had asked her to marry him but she turned him down in favor of Daniel.

---

[4] Hardin County Clerk's Office, Elizabethtown, Hardin County, Kentucky, Deed Book G, 213-14.

On June 12, 1806, Thomas Lincoln instead married Nancy Hanks, who gave birth to the future president on February 12, 1809, in a small log cabin that was then within the bounds of Hardin County, now situated in neighboring Larue County. In 1816 the Lincoln family moved to Indiana. In 1819, after his wife died and he heard that Sally was a widow, Thomas Lincoln returned to Elizabethtown to ask her again to marry him and this time she agreed. A plaque in Elizabethtown marks the site of their wedding, which took place on December 2, 1819, in a larger log house that once stood on North Main Street, adjacent to Sarah Johnston's little cabin.

Sarah Bush Johnston Lincoln; from Coffin's *Abraham Lincoln* (1892).

Our third Lincoln connection involves the great man himself and, in this case, not Samuel Haycraft, Sr., but rather his son and my 4th Great-Granduncle, Samuel Haycraft, Jr., who was the longtime clerk of Hardin County and its unofficial historian. In early 1860, Samuel Jr. initiated a brief correspondence with Lincoln that resulted in eleven letters—six from Haycraft and five from Lincoln—passing between the two men. The first was addressed to "Honest Abe" shortly after he won the nomination of the Republican Party at its convention in Chicago. At the time, Samuel Jr. was a Kentucky state senator who had recently delivered a speech in support of erecting a statue of Daniel Boone in Kentucky. Unfortunately, that letter, which included a copy of the speech, has been lost to history, but luckily Lincoln's reply, which refers to Samuel's letter, has survived:

> Springfield, Ills.
> May 28. 1860
> Dear Sir:
> Your recent letter, without date, is received. Also the copy of your speech on the contemplated Daniel Boone monument, which I have not yet had time to read. In the main you are right about my history. My father was Thomas Lincoln, and Mrs Sally Johnston, was his second wife—You are mistaken about my mother—her maiden name was Nancy Hanks—I was no[t] born at Elizabethtown; but my mother's first child, a daughter, two years older than myself, and now long since deceased, was—I was born Feb. 12. 1809, near where Hogginsville now is, then in Hardin County—I do not think I ever saw you, though

I very well know who you are— so well that I recognized your hand-writing, on opening your letter, before I saw the signature. My recollection is that Ben. Helm was first Clerk, that you succeeded him, that Jack Thomas and William Farleigh graduated in the same office, and that your handwritings were all very similar—Am I right?

My father has been dead near ten years; but my step-mother (Mrs. Johnston) is still living— I am really very glad of your letter, and shall be pleased to receive another at any time—

Yours very truly

A. Lincoln[5]

As late as 1965, Samuel Jr.'s second letter to Lincoln was also believed to have been lost, but it wasn't. Today, it is part of the Lincoln Financial Foundation Collection at the Allen County Public Library in Fort Wayne, Indiana.

In this letter, dated May 31, 1860, Samuel Jr. thanked Lincoln for correcting him in regard to the name of the soon-to-be-elected President's mother, confirmed Lincoln's recollection that old Ben Helm, who had recently died at the age of ninety, was Samuel Jr.'s predecessor, and mentioned, in passing, that he (Samuel, Jr.), at age sixty-five, was the future President's senior by fourteen years.

He also informed Lincoln that a portion of the cabin in which he (Lincoln) was born was still standing near Knob Creek, and suggested that he might wish to come to Hardin County for a visit.

---

[5] *Lincoln and the New York Herald: Unpublished Letters of Abraham Lincoln from the Collection of Judd Stewart* (Plainfield, New Jersey: Privately printed, 1907), 9-11.

What Lincoln looked like when he wrote to Samuel Haycraft, Jr.; courtesy Library of Congress.

He concluded by remarking that his state senatorial term was nearly up and that he did not expect to run for public office again, but rather, to spend his time growing fruit, which he enjoyed doing and was knowledgeable about. In an effort, no doubt, to assure Lincoln that he shared his political point-of-view, Samuel Jr. informed him that, like the future president, he was a former Whig.

In reply, Lincoln wrote:

Hon. Saml. Haycraft.
Springfield, Ills.
June 4, 1860
Dear Sir: Your second letter, dated May 31st. is received. You suggest that a visit to the place of my nativity might be pleasant. Indeed it would. But would it be safe? Would not the people Lynch me?

The place on Knob Creek, mentioned by Mr. Read, I remember very well; but I was not born there. As my parents have told me, I was born on Nolin, very much nearer Hodgin's-Mill than the Knob Creek place is. My earliest recollection, however, is of the Knob Creek place.

Like yourself I belonged to the whig party from it's origin to it's close. I never belonged to the American party organization; nor ever to a party called a Union party; though I hope I neither am, or ever have been, less devoted to the Union than yourself, or any other patriotic man.

It may not be altogether without interest to let you know that my wife is a daughter of the late Robert S. Todd, of Lexington Ky---and that a half sister of hers is the wife of Ben. Hardin Helm, born and raised at your town, but residing at Louisville now, as I believe.

Yours very truly
A. LINCOLN.[6]

On August 16, 1860, Lincoln wrote again:

Hon. Saml. Haycraft
Springfield, Ills.
Aug. 16. 1860

---

[6] John G. Nicolay and John Hay, *Complete Works of Abraham Lincoln, Vol. VI* (Lincoln Memorial University, 1894), 39.

My dear Sir: A correspondent of the New-York Herald, who was here a week ago, writing to that paper, represents me as saying I had been invited to visit Kentucky, but that I suspected it was a trap to inveigle me into Kentucky, in order to do violence to me.

This is wholly a mistake. I said no such thing. I do not remember, but possibly I did mention my correspondence with you. But very certainly I was not guilty of stating, or insinuating, a suspicion of any intended violence, deception, or other wrong, against me, by you, or any other Kentuckian. Thinking this Herald correspondence might fall under your eye, I think it due to myself to enter my protest against the correctness of this part of it. I scarcely think the correspondent was malicious; but rather that he misunderstood what was said.

Yours very truly
A. LINCOLN.[7]

Here is Samuel Haycraft, Jr.'s third (and rather lengthy) reply to Lincoln, which today is preserved in the Library of Congress, Washington, D.C.

Elizabeth Town, Ky
August 19 1860
My dear Sir:
Your letter of 16 Inst was received by this days mail, and I hasten to reply not only to acquit you but to clear myself of any knowledge of the statement of some correspondent in the N. Y. Herald saying that you had been invited to visit Ky., but that you suspected it was a trap to inveigle you into Ky in order to do violence to you."

I will tax your patience by adverting to our correspondence. It was generally understood that you were born in this Town (Elizabeth Town) and as there was some difference of opinion about the place &

---

[7] Ibid., 51.

also about your parentage, that I took the liberty of writing to you on the subject, to which you frankly & promptly responded.

That letter called out another from me, in which I did not invite you to visit Kentucky, but in speaking of the place of your birth & of your recollections of the old Homestead, I made a passing suggestion that it might be pleasant for you now in the turn of life to visit the scenes of your nativity. To which in your letter marked Private dated June 4th you use this playful language "You suggest that a visit to the place of my nativity would be pleasant to me—Indeed it would—But would it be safe? Would not the people Lynch me! The place on Knob Creek marked by Mr Read I remember very well, but I was not born there. As my parents have told me, I was born on Nolin very much nearer Hodgens Mill than the Knob Creek place is—My earliest recollection however is of the Knob-Creek place"

The remark about the Lynching no man of sense would have understood it in any other way than a little playfulness & pleasantry on your part—I at least so understood it, and was about to reply to it in the same humor, that a visit here would subject you to a good many assaults—But they would be for office under you, as it was regarded as a foregone conclusion that you would be the next Prest. Unless the split in the Democratic party let in Bell. The mark Private on your letter I supposed simply meant that it was not for publication, had it been marked confidential, no body would have seen it. But as it was I showed it to Mr. W B Read who was attending our court & one or two other acquaintances & spoke of it to others who like myself had a curiosity about your birthplace

I suppose you have noticed the vote of Ky for clerk of the court of appeals in which the Bell candidate beat the Breckenridge man upward of 25.000 votes. That Breckenridge is in a minority in Ky I have no kind of doubt, but I do not deem the late election a fair test as a great many Douglas men voted for County But I have no doubt that if the parties stand as they are now in Nov. next that Bell & Everett will carry the state of Ky by a considerable plurality of votes—An old neighbor & friend of mine Saml Young told me to say to you if I wrote to you again that he would vote for you, his sister married a Hanks, & he married a sister of my old Friend Charles Sawyer who lives near

Mattoon & who tho near 80 years of age headed a Lincoln torchlight procession at that place not long since & carried a fence rail on his shoulder as did every other man in the procession—Not long since a relative of mine from New York visited this place & aided by several old citizens hunted up the remains of the old cabin in which your father resided. He had 8 feet of a log sawed out & took it to New York The old house has been removed several times. Was once a human residence twice a slaughter house & now a stable.—excuse me for going into these little particulars. I thought you would not be displeased to hear of them—I have seen in the illustrated papers a likeness of yourself—I was almost on the point of saying that if you had a current Photograph of yourself that I would like to see it.

    I do not suppose that you intend to visit Ky But if you do I would like to see you personally and would be surety that you would be pleasantly receivd—I wish it understood that this letter is private & not for publication, but if you desire a reply from me to the N Y Herald I will with pleasure prepare a statement.

    Truly yours
    Saml Haycraft[8]

Lincoln's reply, dated August 23, 1860 was as brief as Haycraft's previous letter had been long.

Springfield, Ills.
August 23, 1860
Hon. Samuel Haycraft,
Elizabethtown, Ky.
My Dear Sir:
    Yours of the 19th just received. I now fear I may have given you some uneasiness by my last letter. I did not mean to intimate that I had, to any extent, been involved or embarrassed by you; nor yet to draw from you anything to relieve myself from

---

[8] Library of Congress, Washington, D.C., Abraham Lincoln papers: Series 1. General Correspondence. 1833-1916: Samuel Haycraft to Abraham Lincoln, Sunday, August 19, 1860.

difficulty. My only object was to assure you that I had not, as represented by the Herald correspondent, charged you with an attempt to inveigle me into Kentucky to do me violence. I believe no such thing of you or of Kentuckians generally; and I dislike to be represented to them as slandering them in any way.
    Yours very truly,
    A. Lincoln.[9]

Here is Samuel Haycraft, Jr.'s fourth letter to Lincoln, which is likewise held by the Library of Congress, Washington, D.C.:

Elizabeth Town, Ky
Oct 26. 1860
My dear Sir
    Not long since I saw my old friend Dick Wintersmith who informed me that he in company with Ben Hardin Helm had lately paid you a visit & taken tea at your house— Dick was our late Treasurer & is a fellow of rare wit & humour & told me that he had expressed his fears to your lady that if it was known in the South that he had supped at your house that he would be hung— I told Dick that I had some fears myself that if you were elected that it would be the cause of my death—How so? Says Dick I replied that Lincoln would give an appointment on [illegible] and Swampy Country among the Indians & that the consequences would be fatal. I have a great curiosity to know how a man feels in your present position. A candidate for the highest office is the gift of a mighty nation & in less than two weeks of the time—I have myself in days past had some anxiety about some petty office But [illegible] in your case is a deep one—In Kentucky, tho a slave state, we occupy a middle ground—and generally we are as much opposed to the fire eating southern disunion gang, as we are to the Ultra

---

[9] Nicolay and Hay, *Complete Works*, 51-2.

abolitionists of the North—From late indications we look upon your election as a fixed fact, a foregone conclusion.—Bell will certainly carry Kentucky & Tennessee as I once before remarked to you—Old Uncle Sammy Young requested me if ever I wrote to you again to be certain to send you his respects—he will vote for you if he lives—one of our Townsmen Robert L Wintersmith is the Lincoln Elector for this District, and takes decided ground—and regrets that he is not an orator that he might canvass the state for you.

Mr. James L. Hill, the son of one of the best women in creation sends you his respects. His mothers maiden name was Lucy Lincoln a daughter of Annanis Lincoln who she says was a brother of yor father—

James L Hills, or as we call him Wheeler Hills, is our industrious enterprising cabinet maker with a tolerably fair education I make these suggestions to you supposing that they might interest or amuse you to a limited extent—. But as no doubt your correspondants are now numerous I must apologize for this letter on light matters, as intruding upon your time. With the highest respects,
Your Obt. Svt.
Saml. Haycraft[10]

Before he received a reply from Lincoln, Haycraft wrote again:

Elizabeth Town Hardin Co Ky
November 9, 1860
Hon. A Lincoln,

Dear Sir,

---

[10] Library of Congress, Washington, D.C., Abraham Lincoln papers: Series 1. General Correspondence. 1833-1916: Samuel Haycraft to Abraham Lincoln, Friday, October 26, 1860.

Now that the Battle is ended and the smoke thereof is being blown away and that you are now beyond doubt President elect of these glorious United States, as I predicted six months ago, I feel inclined though an humble individual unknown to fame to address you a few lines for which I hope you will pardon me, a great weight of responsibility has now fallen on your shoulders, and the guidance of the Ship of State committed to your hand.

I pray God that you may be enabled manfully to bear up under that weight and skillfully to pilot the vessel through the breakers of the threatened storm, that you will in all the honesty of your heart do so I have an abiding confidence, and that our Southern fire eaters will find (if they give you time to show your hand) that you are a conservative chief of the Nation in a national point of view that is the President of the United States and not a sectional ruler. Altho Kentucky gave you but a small vote, you will find her clinging on to the union, and honestly aiding you in the very arduous duties that lie before you. It will no doubt require all your wisdom and skill to conduct the Ship of State through the breakers, and it should be the duty, and I hope will be the pleasure of all good and true men to stand by you in the Conflict. And I hope that all may be well and the unity of the States preserved. This Hot Spring of the South will no doubt try a while to kick up a dust but sober second thought calms them down into decent acquiesence to the choice of the Nation. I do not profess to have the wisdom or the ability to suggest a course of policy. But your prudence and that proper decent respect which you have during the Canvass shown to the dignity of the office to which the people have elevated you without your compromising the respect for the opinions of an enlightened Nation — Stumping the States and harranging the people for an office of the highest dignity will lead you to a course (. . .) and conservative in your administration—is the ground work of my hope for the future.

These remarks are timidly made and I hope you will not think me presumptious or obtrusive in making them. If an outsider may be allowed the privilege, I would name one man in a small way deserving of your patronage, and I make the suggestion without his knowledge or (. . .). I mean our fellow citizen (of this Town) Mr. Robert L. Wintersmith who was one on your electoral ticket. He stood almost alone and advocated your claim. And I have heard but one sentiment among the people and that is that he ought to be remembered while favors are being dispensed. He has labored through adverse fortune with a large family and is poor, but as firm as the Rock of Gibralter.

I expect you will be annoyed to decide with letters and all sorts of petitions and communications from your own supporters, and I can hardly expect any reply to this communication, indeed it may be considered impertinent under all circumstances; but it is not so intended, and is made in the honesty of my heart. It is true that I would like to hear from you if your leisure permits.

Very Respectfully Yours,
Saml Haycraft[11]

Lincoln's fifth and final letter to Haycraft, marked "Private and Confidential," was the briefest of all:

Springfield, Illinois,
November 13, 1860.
Hon. Samuel Haycraft.

My dear Sir:
Yours of the 9th is just received. I can only answer briefly. Rest fully assured that the good people of the South who will put themselves in the same temper and mood toward me which you do, will find no cause to complain of me.

---

[11] Library of Congress, Washington, D.C., Abraham Lincoln papers: Series 1. General Correspondence. 1833-1916: Samuel Haycraft to Abraham Lincoln, November 9, 1860.

While I can not, as yet, make any committal as to offices, I sincerely hope I may find it in my power to oblige the friends of Mr. Wintersmith.
Yours very truly,
A. Lincoln.[12]

On the very same day that Lincoln wrote his final letter to Samuel Haycraft, the former county clerk composed his sixth and also final missive to the President-Elect, in which he once again proposed that "Old Abe," as he was popularly known, visit the state of his birth:

Elizabeth Town Ky
Nov 13, 1860
(Private)
Hon. Abraham Lincoln,

Not withstanding my late communication excuse me for troubling you so soon again. My apology will be found in my great desire that you should be disabused before the South and in the Slave States and thereby afford you a smoother sea than the present ebullitions of the South seem to portend. I am satisfied that a very large majority of Kentuckians are (. . .) to your election from the fact that they believe firmly that your administration will be honest, just and conservative. If you read the Louisville Journal you will see a decided tendency in that way, and that paper gives tongue to a very large portion of our people. But to come to the point—It has been intimated to me (knowing that I had been in correspondence with you) that it might serve the public and be promotive of some good for you to pay a visit to Kentucky at this point, being the County of your nativity and make a public address—and it was suggested to me

---

[12] Nicolay and Hay, *Complete Works*, 69-70.

to draw up a call upon you to be signed by all our old citizens giving you a public invitation. But I answered that it would be proper for me first to address you privately on the subject and learn from you confidentially whether such a demonstration would be agreeable to you to meet your notion of propriety. My own opinion is that there would be no impropriety in it as the election is over, and you could have no private ends to answer, and coupled with the fact that before the election you maintained that (. . .) silence which became a candidate for so high a position. I want Ky to speak out in such decisive language of the importance of adhering to the union and Constitution as would leave no doubt about her position and give no hope to the South that she would in the slightest degree encourage the madmen of that Section to look to her for aid, comfort or help in their hairbrained attempt to dissolve the union. I conversed with Governor Helm today on this subject. He highly approves of the plans to get your answer by a visit or such a reply to an invitation as would have a tendency to allay the troubled elements. But as some of his friends about Frankfort and Louisville have spoken of him as likely to obtain some executive favors, in which he has had no (. . .) or expectations in that way will induce him as a modest and high toned gentleman to take no active hand in the arrangements. This I say confidentially—I am confident that a visit from you once arranged would bring a tremendous crowd who would meet you openhanded, and listen to you with pleasure. If you can answer personally please let me hear from you.
    Yours truly
    Saml Haycraft[13]

As it happened, Lincoln never did visit Hardin County, Kentucky. Consequently, he and Samuel Haycraft, Jr. never

---

[13] Library of Congress, Washington, D.C., Abraham Lincoln papers: Series 1. General Correspondence. 1833-1916: Samuel Haycraft to Abraham Lincoln, Friday, November 13, 1860.

met in person, nor was there any further communication between the two men until February 1865, when Kentuckian Charles D. Poston, serving as territorial delegate to Congress from Arizona, wrote to Lincoln, enclosing a letter from Haycraft, which had been sent to him and not directly to Lincoln. Both are now in the Library of Congress, Washington, D.C.

>Washington City
>18. Feby 1865.
>My dear Sir
>I take the liberty of enclosing a letter from Mr Haycraft expressing his regards for you
>I had hoped to have him on at the inauguration but it seems he cannot leave home
>The Old Gentleman has been plundered a good deal both by Rebel and Union troops
>If you could write him a little note by way of protection from the latter it would be a great comfort to his old age, and grateful to your friend and
>Obedient Servant
>Charles D Poston[14]

And here is the letter that Poston enclosed:

>Elizabeth Town Ky
>February 13 1865
>Dear Sir

---

[14] Library of Congress, Washington, D.C., Abraham Lincoln papers: Series 1. General Correspondence. 1833-1916: Charles D. Poston to Abraham Lincoln, Saturday, February 18, 1865 (enclosing letter from Samuel Haycraft).

My thanks for the garden seed I have written to Margaret the most I had to say as I presumed she has more time to read than you have I should be much pleased to visit the city especially for my wife to go, but it seems she can not. I should be pleased to see the President. As I have a considerable fancy for him altho we differ a little about the negro question. But that is all gone up. The Rebellion has used up slavery & it is bound to go. And if it does we will, that is our children will be better off in 20 years and the negros a great deal worse off if not extinct. If you have a chance please present my best regards to the President and particularly for relieving Genl Burbridge from the control of Kentucky. We know nothing of Gen Palmer who succeeds him but we have the Consolation to know that we cannot be worsted by having Genl Burbridge taken away

Kentucky is now suffering sorely from Guerilla bands Burbridge would do nothing to put them down & when Gov Bramlette would try at State expense to raise some troops to defend the state, that Stupid Tyrant & Blockhead Burbridge would have them disbanded. Burbridge is not only a fool, but is a bad man

Yours Truly,
Saml Haycraft

Rev. Mr. Saml Williams, S.B Thomas & others required me to give you thanks for papers documents &c
S H[15]

If Lincoln did as Poston suggested and wrote again to Haycraft, the letter has unfortunately not survived. Chances are that he didn't, in light of all that was happening during the early months of 1865, when the war was finally coming to an end.

---

[15] Ibid.

****

Our family's fourth and final connection to Abraham Lincoln is quite a bit more tenuous than the first three. It also has nothing to do with anyone named Haycraft, although it's still on my mother's side of the family tree.

In 1863, at the height of the Civil War, one of my 4th great-grandmothers, Sarah Ann Reed (née Lowry), better known as "Sallie," lived with the youngest of her adult children in a farmhouse on the east side of West Chickamauga Creek in Catoosa County, Georgia. Sallie's husband, James Jacob Reed, had died three years earlier, in May 1860.

In September of that year, Sallie found herself in the thick of one of the largest and bloodiest military contests of the Civil War—the Battle of Chickamauga—which began when Confederate troops under the command of General Braxton Bragg evacuated nearby Chattanooga, Tennessee in the face of an advancing federal army commanded by General William Rosecrans. Soon after, Bragg and thousands of Confederate soldiers came rushing into the valley through which Chickamauga Creek had previously flowed peacefully (it would later be called "the River of Death"). Entirely by chance, the first skirmish between these retreating troops and their federal pursuers took place at Reed's Bridge, a short wooden plank crossing that spanned the creek near Sarah Reed's farmhouse. The cannon that fired the opening shot of the battle was reportedly positioned in her front yard.[16]

A book that was sold as a souvenir of the 1895 Atlanta Cotton Exposition tells the story of what happened there:

> On the 18th of September was fired the first gun of what is known as the great battle of Chickamauga. The position of the two armies that morning, in brief, was as follows:
>
> Rosecrans occupied the northwest bank of West Chickamauga Creek, his line extending along its sinuous course for a dozen miles or more, guarding all the fords, bridges, or other places of transit, for the purpose of preventing a crossing by the Confederate army.
>
> The Confederates were on the southeast side of the creek, which is very muddy and generally quite deep; and Bragg's idea was to force his way over, at various points, and fight the battle on the Chattanooga side of the Creek.
>
> At Reed's Bridge, in Catoosa county, Ga., some seven miles west of Ringgold, a detachment of Michigan cavalry was stationed, with orders to prevent any advance by the Confederates. Having been there for a day or more, their commander determined, that morning, to send about 200 mounted men across the bridge, for the purpose of making a reconnaissance, and developing the Confederate position. At the same time he ordered that the planks be loosened, so that, when the cavalry returned, these could be dropped into the creek and the bridge thus practically destroyed. The detachment crossed the stream, as ordered, and the work of loosening the planks was commenced by the others.

---

[16] Jos. M. Brown, *Mountain Campaigns of Georgia* (Buffalo, New York: The Matthews-Northup Co., 1895), 13-16.

The fight for Reed's Bridge at the Battle of Chickamauga; from Brown's *Mountain Campaigns of Georgia*.

The scouting party, however, had scarcely begun deploying on the east side of the creek before the Confederates, who had been watching them some couple of hundred yards distant, at the edge of the woods on the summit of the elevation rising from the bridge, opened fire, from a couple of pieces of artillery. The very first discharge secured the range of the bridge, and a bombshell exploding upon it, knocked up some of the planks, and killed one man, and wounded two others. Almost at the same instant a volley of musketry was fired from the same position.

The work of destruction of the bridge by the Federals instantly ceased, and there was a stampede for cover to the forest near by. The detachment 'of cavalry on the east bank, seeing the folly of attempting to cross the bridge under a raking fire, galloped northeastward, down the creek, endeavoring to find some other crossing place. After going about a mile and a half and finding no regular ford, they swam their horses through the stream, and thus escaped.

In the meantime, the Confederates charged across the bridge, dispersed the cavalry, and immediately turned downward, towards Alexander's Bridge, about one mile and a half distant, and, after quite a struggle, possession of this was also secured.

Later on, during the day, crossing was effected at several other points. Accordingly, the next morning found Bragg's army, in line of battle, on the northwest side of West Chickamauga Creek. The struggle then began, which continued with such desperate fury, and resulted in such distressing carnage to both sides, during the next three days.

Bragg's object seems to have been to crush Rosecrans's left wing, and secure possession of the road leading through Missionary Ridge, via Rossville, to Chattanooga. The result of the battle is well known. Rosecrans's army was routed and driven back to Chattanooga; and, but for the stand which General Thomas took, on Snodgrass Hill, and his heroic defence of that position, and the check which he gave to the Confederates at that point, the defeat of Rosecrans would have been a crushing one, and the sweep of the Confederate advance may have extended back to Kentucky, and have almost changed the fate of the war. "But great battles are fought behind the stars."

The Confederates captured 8,000 prisoners, 51 cannon, over 15,000 stand of small arms, about 40 standards, and an enormous amount of army stores. The battlefield was principally in a level, thickly-wooded plain, where it was hard to use artillery with much effect, and where the movements of large bodies of troops were veiled in obscurity. It is stated that there were numerous instances of where portions of one army's line were driven back by its enemy, and these, in turn, would soon find themselves caught by a cross-fire, or almost surrounded by a counter successful movement by the other side.

The strength of Rosecrans's army, during the three days' struggle, was 64,392 men. Bragg opened with 33,583 the first day; but, during the second, was re-enforced by Longstreet's corps, which had just arrived from Virginia, and which made his total force engaged 47,321. Longstreet's troops arrived via the Western & Atlantic Railroad, and deployed from the trains at Ringgold and Greenwood, just below, and hurried into the midst of the fray. As the result of this battle, the Federal army was driven back into Chattanooga; and the Confederates occupied Missionary Ridge and Lookout Mountain, from which latter they could overlook Chattanooga, and by the possession of which they were enabled to break Rosecrans's communications by rail with Nashville. They also re-occupied Bridgeport.[17]

At this point, you might be wondering: *What does any of this have to do with Abraham Lincoln?* Sure, he was President when the battle occurred, but where's the connection? Well, here it is: One of the Confederate casualties of Chickamauga was General Ben Hardin Helm of Kentucky, who was married to Emelie Todd, half-sister of Mary Todd Lincoln. Thus, he was Lincoln's brother-in-law. After Helm received a mortal wound on the battlefield, he was taken to the Reed farmhouse, which had been converted into a makeshift Confederate field hospital by General Breckinridge. According to family lore, Sarah Lowry Reed nursed the wounded general herself before he died late that evening.[18]

---

[17] Ibid.
[18] Reed, Descendants of Jacob Reed [http://www.angelfire.com/ga4/jholc/Reed.html; accessed 8 June

General Ben Hardin Helm, Abraham Lincoln's brother-in-law, who died in Sarah Lowry Reed's farmhouse while reportedly being tended by her; from Wikipedia.

****

There is an interesting epilogue to this story. In December 1863, on her way home to Kentucky following General Helm's death at Chickamauga, his widow, Mrs. Emilie Todd Helm, visited President and Mrs. Lincoln at the

---

2010].

White House, where she "was received...with every sign of affection and kindness."[19] Mrs. Helm later wrote:

> I told Mr. Lincoln...that I did not intend to embarrass him or make myself conspicuous in any way, in case he allowed me to proceed to my home in Kentucky. I was his guest for several days; when I left he gave me a paper worded to protect me in person and property (except as to slaves), and as I thanked him he said, "I have known you all your life, and I never knew you to do a mean thing."[20]

Not surprisingly, Mrs. Helm's White House visit created quite a stir, especially in the press, but Lincoln seems to have shrugged it off as of no consequence. After all, he had more important matters to deal with, such as the conduct of the war. That did not mean, however, that Mrs. Helm was entirely forgotten, nor given unlimited leniency on account of being family. In August 1864, Lincoln sent the following message to General Stephen G. Burbridge, military commander of the Commonwealth of Kentucky. It reads as follows:

WAR DEPARTMENT, WASHINGTON, D.C.
August 8, 1864
MAJOR-GENERAL BURBRIDGE, Lexington, Ky.:

---

[19] "President Lincoln and the Widow of General Helms," The Century Magazine, vol. 52, No. 2, June 1896, 318.
[20] Ibid.

Last December Mrs. Emily T. Helm, half-sister of Mrs. L., and widow of the rebel general Ben. Hardin Helm, stopped here on her way from Georgia to Kentucky, and I gave her a paper, as I remember, to protect her against the mere fact of her being General Helm's widow. I hear a rumor to-day that you recently sought to arrest her, but was prevented by her presenting the paper from me. I do not intend to protect her against the consequences of disloyal words or acts spoken or done by her since her return to Kentucky, and if the paper given her by me can be construed to give her protection for such words or acts, it is hereby revoked pro tanto. Deal with her current conduct just as you would with any other.

A. LINCOLN[21]

---

[21] Ibid.

The Riot at Purdy

It's often been remarked that the Civil War not only divided the nation but also families, turning father against son, son against father, brother against brother, and so on. I doubt there's any better illustration of this unfortunate consequence than my second great-grandfather, Daniel P. Seay, and his uncle—my third great-granduncle—Samuel Lewis, Jr., who fought on opposite sides in Western Tennessee.

While Dan Seay was out riding with the Sixteenth Tennessee Cavalry, C.S.A, which was part of a larger force commanded by Confederate Gen. Nathan Bedford Forrest, his uncle—the oldest brother of Dan's mother, Elizabeth Lewis Seay—served with a Union cavalry unit the goal of which was to curtail General Forrest's activities in Western Tennessee. It is not hard to imagine that these conflicting allegiances must have put a considerable strain on the relationship between the two families, and it must have been particularly difficult for Elizabeth Lewis Seay. I can't help but wonder: Who did she side with? Her son, or her brother? And did she ever worry that in the heat of battle, one might kill the other?

It's no exaggeration to say, as one author did, that during this period of history, "Human life was held exceedingly cheap...and especially in west Tennessee; the scenes of bloodshed which stained this section of the South may well suggest the reddest days of the French Revolution."[1] By and large, the fault for this state of affairs was laid at the feet of its principal military leaders, both of who were allegedly harsh and brutal men.

Unsurprisingly, Northerners blamed General Forrest, whose Mississippi men had killed scores of both black and white soldiers after they reportedly threw down their weapons and surrendered at Fort Pillow, Tennessee. The "Fort Pillow Massacre," as it was thereafter called, which occurred on April 12, 1864, served as a prime example of Confederate, and particularly General Forrest's, cruelty.[2] A postwar biographer of the controversial general tried to downplay the episode (and others) by saying that the Civil War had "a deplorable effect upon the morals of the rank and file of either army." Furthermore, he remarked, it did "not bring out the noblest traits of the majority of those who from choice or necessity follow[ed] its blood-stained paths." The result, he opined, was that "Too often the better qualities hide away, and those that are harsh and cruel prevail." That being said, he laid most of the blame squarely upon the federals, adding:

---

[1] John Allen Wyeth, *Life of Lieutenant-General Nathan Bedford Forrest* (New York and London: Harper & Brothers, Publishers, 1908), 368.
[2] *The Lancaster Examiner*, Lancaster, Pennsylvania, April 20, 1864.

> Some of Forrest's men treasured a deep resentment…They had been neighbors in times of peace, and had taken opposite sides when the war came on. These men had suffered violence to person and property, and their wives and children, in the enforced absence of their natural protectors, had suffered various indignities at the hands of the "Tennessee Tories," as the loyal Tennesseeans were called by their neighbors who sided with the South. When they met in single combat, or in scouting parties, or in battle, as far as these individuals were concerned, it was too often a duel to the death. Between the parties to these neighborhood feuds the laws of war did not prevail. Here, in this melee, in the fire and excitement of the assault, they found opportunity and made excuse for bloody vengeance.[3]

Unfortunately, there is some truth to the accusation of "indignities at the hands of the 'Tennessee Tories.'" The regiment to which Sam Lewis, Jr. was attached, the Sixth Tennessee Cavalry, was led by Colonel Fielding Hurst, a steadfast unionist and the largest landholder in McNairy County, where both the Seay and Lewis families lived. Ironically, Hurst was a slave-owner! He was also, from all accounts, the sort of man you either loved or hated. Oftentimes operating without restraint or federal authority, Colonel Hurst's reportedly harsh methods of dealing with both Confederates and Confederate sympathizers led his men to be derisively damned as "Hurst's Worst."

If you wish to know more about the activities of General Forrest and his troops in Western Tennessee, Southern

---

[3] Wyeth, *Life of Lieutenant-General Nathan Bedford Forrest*, 368.

Kentucky, and Northern Mississippi during the Civil War, there are a number of books from which to choose. A book that tells the story of Colonel Wurst and his command has also been published, and I urge you to seek these out, but this is a story about one particular soldier and what happened to him during the war, and also, the tragedy that befell him and his family after it was over. Therefore, dear reader, if you don't mind, I'll focus on him.

Sam Lewis, Jr.'s military service began on August 11, 1862, at Bethel, Tennessee, where he enlisted for three-years as a private in Company A, First Regiment of West Tennessee Cavalry, later reorganized as the Sixth Tennessee Cavalry.

In contrast to his Confederate nephew, who was single and not yet out of his teens, at the time Sam Jr. enlisted, he was thirty-six-years-old and married, with six children and one more on the way. William, Sam's oldest son, wasn't much younger than his cousin Dan.

Sam's compiled service record reveals that his rise through the ranks was nothing short of meteoric, at least at first. On October 1, 1862, he was promoted to Sergeant. A little more than two months later, on December 15, 1862, he was advanced to the rank of Second Lieutenant. On July 1, 1863, by order of Colonel Hurst, he was promoted to First Lieutenant. On October 5, 1863, he was placed in command of his company, but not promoted. In December 1863, he was detached to serve at a court martial.

It appears that by and large, Sam enjoyed good health during his term of service, that is until April 5, 1864, when he was admitted to the officers' hospital at Memphis, Tennessee. Whatever his ailment, it couldn't have been too serious because by May, he was in command of his company again. A muster card for July and August 1864 includes the notation: "Commanded company from 5th Oct. 1863 to present date & have been the responsible officer & camp & garrison & equipage & has received no pay for responsibilities during that time." His service record does not indicate whether or not that oversight, in terms of pay, was ever corrected, but on November 21, 1864, at Memphis, he was at last promoted to Captain.

Unlike the Confederate unit in which Sam's young nephew served, the activities of the Sixth Tennessee Cavalry, almost all of which took place in Western Tennessee—territory that was "home" to Sam—have also been well-documented, both in newspapers of the time, as well as official government records of the Civil War.

Unfortunately, some of these records confirm that accusations of misbehavior, on the part of federal troops in West Tennessee—most often looting and misappropriation of civilian property—were not entirely unfounded, although it should be noted too that these depredations were not always the work of so-called "Tennessee Tories." In September 1863, for example, after the Sixth Cavalry entered the town of Grand Junction, in Hardeman County,

Lt. Col. William E. M. Breckenridge discovered that some of the town's citizens were giving whiskey by the bucketful to his prisoners. After going "over to where they were" and having "the whisky all spilled" that he could find, he ordered Sam Lewis to take ten men and "destroy all the liquor they could find" in the town.[4]

"In a short time," recalled Breckenridge, Lt. Lewis "came to me and said that the men were breaking into the houses," whereupon "I ordered him to go and stop them, and to arrest every man be found in a house. He then went off, and in a short time returned and told me of Mrs. A. A. Newman's millinery shop or store, and I ordered him to put a guard over the house." Breckenridge went on to write:

> There were a good many stragglers around town, and after dark I and another officer of the command, I do not know his name or regiment, heard a noise at a door, and started to see about it, and on the way I found about 30 men, I suppose, in and in front of a store. He said they belonged to his regiment, and I ordered them out, and the owner then shut the door and we went on, and in a few minutes returned; they were trying to get in again. I sent the officer to send them off, and I spent the most of my time that night in running from place to place trying to keep everything quiet and seeing to the wounded. And in the morning, when Colonel Hatch returned to town, the men broke open houses and took all they wanted, command pass, and nearly every man had something that had been taken out of the place and took buggies and wagons and loaded them with goods and boots, &c. I stood in the court-house yard and saw a portion

---

[4] The *Miscellaneous Documents of the House of Representatives for the First Session of the Fifty-First Congress, 1889-'90* (Washington, D.C.: Government Printing Office, 1891), 679.

of his command pass, and nearly every man had something that had been taken out of the place.[5]

Sam Lewis' report of the matter makes it clear that the troublemakers were not Tennesseans.

>GRAND JUNCTION, TENN., October 4, 1863.
>I was in command of my company, and was held back in charge of some prisoners. When the regiment advanced, I moved up into the edge of town. Colonel Breckenridge being informed by a citizen that the citizens were giving our men whisky, Colonel Breckenridge ordered me to take some men and proceed to all suspicious places in town and destroy all the whisky I could find; and while I was searching for whisky, I went into one store belonging to a widow lady, and found her very much excited about the soldiers carrying out her goods. She demanded of me a guard. I went to Colonel Breckenridge and related her circumstances to him, and he told me to give her a guard. I then advanced to the court-house and took charge of the prisoners, with James J. Smith, lieutenant of the same company. I remained there all night writing paroles for prisoners. Next morning, I went out some distance north of the court house, where the wounded were, and fell in company with Colonel Hurst. We had a conversation about the way the soldiers were treating the citizens. He ordered me to go and tell my men not to interrupt anything in town. As I was returning to my command, I saw Colonel Hatch's men, of the Third Michigan, or the Second Iowa Cavalry, breaking open storehouse doors and carrying out goods of almost every description.
>SAMUEL LEWIS
>Lieutenant Company A, Sixth Tennessee Cavalry Volunteers[6]

---

[5] Ibid.

[6] Ibid., 679-80.

In late May 1865, a little more than a month after Lee's surrender at Appomattox, Captain Samuel Lewis, Jr. resigned his commission, and on June 3, he was officially discharged. As soon as possible, no doubt, he returned home to his family, which by this time included two-year-old Margaret.

Shortly after his return home in 1865, Sam Lewis was appointed sheriff of McNairy County, an unenviable, thankless job at any time, but especially so during those volatile postwar years when the wounds of war were still raw and the desire to settle old scores was rife, especially among ex-Confederates who found themselves on the losing side of a great national struggle. Making matters worse, at least insofar as former rebels were concerned, Tennessee was governed during the years immediately following the war by a former Methodist minister and Radical Republican named William G. Brownlow, a man who Sheriff Sam Lewis wholeheartedly supported. This was during the era when the Republicans were the liberal, not the conservative party of the nation, and champions of equal rights for all citizens, not just the white ones.

It should never be forgotten that the Confederacy fought to protect and perpetuate not only the South's "peculiar institution" but also white supremacy. Consequently, even though the abolition of slavery had been achieved by ratification of the thirteenth amendment in 1865, which meant that there was no going back to slavery, the thought of political and social equality with former slaves, people that most white antebellum Southerners had been taught from birth to consider their inferiors, was anathema to nearly anyone who had fought under the stars and bars. It's almost certainly no coincidence that in the same year—1867—that Governor Brownlow ushered through a state law enfranchising the freedmen of Tennessee, Nathan Bedford Forrest founded the Ku Klux Klan. That's why what happened to Sam Lewis, Jr., who approved of Governor Brownlow's policies, is so terribly ironic. If he had been an unreconstructed Southerner, what happened to him when the war was over would have made sense, *but he wasn't, and it didn't.*

Former Confederates were also incensed by the Governor's acceptance of former slaves into the state militia, which he caused to be stationed at various places around the state, ostensibly to maintain order. Not surprisingly, unrepentant Tennesseans everywhere denounced this action claiming that it was the militia, not ordinary citizens, who were responsible for most disorderly acts. The following editorial, published in the Winchester *Home Journal* (Franklin County, Tennessee) in 1867 is typical:

> We cannot, for the life of us, by all that is true and in the fear of God—we cannot see how any honest man, with any soul—with any regard for an impoverished, law-abiding people, could assert that there was the faintest shadow of necessity for

a standing army, composed mainly of outlaws, in our midst. In all the breadth and length of Tennessee, the most perfect submission there was to Radical rule, and all reports to the contrary were gotten up by Radicals for party purpose. In the county of Franklin the first murder was committed by Capt. Rickman's men on a citizen named Brown. Houses were robbed and citizens insulted, but until Brownlow's militia were called out, all was quiet.[7]

Tennessee Governor W. G. Brownlow; from Sketches of the Rise, Progress and Decline of Secession (1862).

---

[7] *Home Journal*, Winchester, Tennessee, June 27, 1867.

PROCLAMATION
By the Governor of the State of Tennessee.

Whereas, It has been made known to me, the Governor of the State of Tennessee, that certain atrocious murders and numerous outrages have been committed in certain counties in this State, by violent and disloyal men, whose only offence has been their unswerving devotion to the National Flag, and their uniform support of the State Government; and whereas, these bad men are banding themselves together in some localities, and notifying loyal men to leave within a given time. Now, therefore, I, WILLIAM G. BROWNLOW, Governor, as aforesaid, by virtue of the authority and power in me vested, do hereby solemnly proclaim, that I intend to put a stop to all such outrages, by at once calling into actual service a sufficient number of loyal volunteers, under the following recent act, which is now the law of Tennessee:

An Act to organize and equip a State Guard, and for other purposes.

Be it enacted by the General Assembly of the State of Tennessee, That the Governor is hereby authorized and empowered to organize, equip and call into active service a volunteer force to be known as the Tennessee State Guard, to be composed of one or more regiments from each Congressional District of the State: Provided, always, that the Tennessee State Guard shall be composed of loyal men, who shall take and subscribe the oath prescribed in the Franchise Act.

Sec. 2. *Be it further enacted,* That the Governor shall be Commander-in-Chief, and any member of said force shall be subject to his order, when in his opinion the safety of life, property, liberty or the faithful execution of law require it; to be organized, armed, equipped, regulated and governed by the rules and articles of war and the revised army regulations of the United States, so far as applicable, and shall receive pay and allowances according to grade of rank, as provided for the United States army while as active service, to be paid out of any money in the State Treasury not otherwise appropriated: Provided, that the force provided for this act shall not be armed and equipped until called into active service by the Governor.

Sec. 3. *Be it further enacted,* That this act shall take effect from and after its passage.

Brownlow's proclamation regarding the militia; from the *East Tennessee Union Flag*, March 29, 1867.

Unfortunately, only a month or so after the above diatribe was published, Tennesseans who resented Governor Brownlow's Radical policies were able to point the finger and say, "I told you so!"

This newspaper report, which was published in *The Bolivar Bulletin*. (Bolivar, Hardeman County, Tennessee.), on Aug. 3, 1867, explains what happened:

> Last Saturday, one week ago today, a serious difficulty occurred at Purdy, McNairy county. From reliable sources we gather the following in regard to the affray. Thirty negro militia, under command of one Hamilton, is stationed there. On the day of the difficulty, eight or ten of the militia were in town; they offered violence to a freedman from the country; Senator John Aldridge, radical, seeing that the militia were imposing upon the freedman, endeavored to persuade them that what they were doing was wrong; failing to accomplish his purpose, he called upon Samuel Lewis, sheriff of the county, and who was, during the war, a captain in Col. Hurst's 6th Tennessee regiment. Lewis came promptly to the call, and while endeavoring, in a peaceable, yet determined manner, to discharge his duty, he was fired on and mortally wounded. This somewhat enraged one of his former comrades-in-arms, who drew his pistol and shot the militiaman in the face; the shot was returned by the squad, and two white men were severely, if not dangerously wounded. Great excitement prevailed, during which the militia returned to their quarters, but on Sunday they again came into town and renewed the disturbance, by shooting into houses and firing at almost every living thing they saw. Many persons left the place and are still absent from their homes.[8]

---

[8] *The Bolivar Bulletin*. (Bolivar, Tennessee.), August 3, 1867.

Another version of the incident, published in a Memphis newspaper, used similar, and in some places, identical language. It differed however, by taking the opportunity not only to point out the irony of Sheriff Lewis' death at the hands of a black militia man but also to criticize the Governor.

THE RIOT AT PURDY
The Radicals Unable to Control the Negroes
A Radical Sheriff Killed
Terrible Condition of Things

In the riot at Purdy, on Saturday last, we learn from a source that cannot be questioned, that Samuel Lewis, the Sheriff of the county, was killed and three others white men wounded. Lewis was an ex-Federal officer, a kind-hearted man, and served with credit as captain of cavalry in the late war. He was a Radical, and unwavering in his support of Brownlow. At the time of his death, he was endeavoring to keep the peace, and to arrest a drunken negro who was disturbing the same by quarreling with another gentleman of color. He fell in the discharge of his duty. Just as Lewis was shot, a white Radical friend fired at the murderer and wounded him slightly. A free fight then began. The negro militia swept the town, and were perfectly furious. They shot into houses filled with women and children, poured a merciless volley at unarmed citizens, and inaugurated a reign of terror never known before in that little village. Prominent Radicals tried to stop them, but they were utterly unable to control them. Radicalism is dethroned by its own minions. Judge Hurst, to his honor be it said, was active in behalf of law and order, but the negroes would not heed him. Since the murderous affray, the "melish" have patrolled the town at night, and amused themselves by shooting into private dwellings. The citizens, old and young, have abandoned their houses, and the solitude of once happy homes is only broken by the brutal tread of Brownlow's negro ruffians. In the name of Heaven, will the people support Wm. G. Brownlow, who is the real author of these atrocities? Is it not a striking fact that Samuel Lewis was murdered by the very power that his Radical friends (perhaps he was guilty) had summoned to Purdy to oppress Conservatives and so-called rebels.[9]

Another paper, *The Bolivar Bulletin*, opined:

> While at the junction last Tuesday we heard a dozen gentlemen, some them radicals, eulogize the manly deeds of Mr. Lewis, all agreed that he was a gallant soldier, firm friend, good neighbor, and an honest man, even though he was a radical. The two additional whites who were wounded, were also radicals and members of the old Tennessee regiment. Verily, "he who sows the wind shall reap the whirlwind."[10]

At this point you may well be wondering: Who was the man that shot Sam Lewis and what happened to him? The answer to the first question is James Hardin, "a pestilent disturber of the peace in those parts," said one newspaper. The answer to the second question is that presumably, he was immediately arrested and thrown into jail.[11]

And then there's the question: What about Sheriff Lewis' family? What happened to them? Whenever I think of his widow, Martisia, left with nine mostly young children (including an infant) to raise, I can't help but picture in my

---
[9] *Memphis Daily Avalanche*, Memphis, Tennessee, August 1, 1867.
[10] The Bolivar Bulletin, Bolivar, Tennessee, August 3, 1867.
[11] *The Tennessean*, Nashville, Tennessee, December 21, 1867.

mind that poor sheriff's wife, played by actress Sally Fields in the movie, "Places in the Heart," which chronicles a similar tragedy. Did Sam Lewis' friends, as in the movie, bring the sheriff's dead body into his house and lay him out on his kitchen table so that his grieving wife could see for herself that he was really dead and prepare him for burial? Perhaps, but of course I don't know for sure.

Fortunately, two of the Lewis boys, William and Wiley, were old enough for farm work, which was almost certainly a great help to their mother. The federal pension that Martisia later applied for and received helped the family financially, but of course it was no replacement for her husband.

On December 21, 1867, presumably after spending months in the McNairy County jail, James Hardin, the accused killer of Sam Lewis was formally charged with murder. The *Nashville Tennessean* predicted that because so many "rebel" whites were then disenfranchised and therefore ineligible to sit on a jury, it was likely that an all-black jury would be chosen, almost certainly resulting in a verdict of not guilty.[12] Is this what happened?

The answer to that question is "no." Why? Because for some reason that has been lost to history, on April 13, 1868, when the case was finally ready to be heard in circuit court, presided over by Judge Fielding Hurst, Samuel Lewis'

---

[12] Ibid.

former commanding officer, the attorney general who prosecuted for the state entered a plea of *nolle prosequi*, which meant he no longer wished to pursue the case. In short: *There was no trial*.

Whether he agreed with this course of action or not, Judge Hurst had no choice but to order that Hardin be released and the jurors paid for their time. At the same session of the court, the attorney general also declined to pursue a charge of rioting against five men, two of who bore the surname Hurst, but apparently were no relation to the judge. I speculate that these five men were some of Governor Brownlow's militia men, but I don't know for sure. Was there some connection between these two cases? And why did the state not go ahead with prosecuting either Hardin or these alleged rioters? After all, there were plenty of eyewitnesses. However, once again, I must say "I don't know." Unfortunately, there are a great many seemingly unanswerable questions about this case due to an apparent lack of records.

In any event, James Hardin was soon back out on the streets of Purdy, but if there was anyone who felt that justice had been thwarted, and surely there were some, most notably Sam Lewis' family, they did not have to wait too long for fate to intervene.

The following report, which appeared on February 11, 1869 in the *Nashville Union and American* explains what happened:

> A negro named James Hardin was at a dance given by the colored people of McNairy county a few nights since, and fired upon a party of serenaders who were enjoying themselves at the ball. The serenaders returned the fire, killing Hardin. The Jackson *Tribune* says that Hardin will be recollected as the murderer of Samuel Lewis, the sheriff of McNairy county in 1867, which event induced a terrible riot in Purdy between the whites and blacks, in which the colored gentleman "fit" nobly and came out victoriously. Since that time, Hardin has been, to some extent, a terror to the community. No whites were implicated in his taking off.[13]

Today, James Hardin is an obscure footnote on the pages of history, but the name of Samuel Lewis, Jr., the first law enforcement officer of McNairy County, Tennessee to lose his life in the performance of his duties, has not been forgotten. It can be found on Panel 11E: 21 of the National Law Enforcement Officers Memorial, which stands in the center of the 400 block of E Street, NW, Washington, D.C. The memorial, which was dedicated on October 15, 1991, commemorates federal, state, and local law enforcement officers who have died in the line of duty.

And if you are ever passing through Southwestern Tennessee, you can stop and pay your respects at the grave of Sam Lewis, Jr., who was buried at the Buena Vista Church Cemetery in Bethel, McNairy County, Tennessee. Just look for the upright Union veterans' tombstone, placed there in 1891, to call attention to his military service in the

---

[13] *The Nashville Union and American*, Nashville, Tennessee, February 11, 1869.

Civil War, a war that ended slavery and fulfilled President Abraham Lincoln's aim of preserving the Union.

Martisia Lewis never remarried. After raising her children to adulthood, she continued to live in McNairy County until her own death, sometime after 1900.

Uncle Jack and the U-Boat

I am sorry to say I did not know my Uncle Jack Jenkins very well. Although he lived in the same county, he never visited us when I was a kid and we rarely if ever, visited him either. For most of my life, and his, I can truthfully (but regretfully) say that if I had passed him on the street on any day, I probably wouldn't have recognized him and it's likely he wouldn't have recognized me either.

Although I may have seen him when I was young and just don't remember, there are two times I clearly recollect and both occurred long after I was fully grown. One of these was when my mother asked me to drive her to his home in Grand Prairie, Texas, so that she could see him. This was in 1984. At the time, he was recovering from a heart operation and she was worried about him, especially since she had not seen him in a long time. The next time I saw Uncle Jack was sixteen years later, when he and I both attended my Uncle Lindell's funeral. (See next chapter for more about Lindell.) In short, Uncle Jack just wasn't the type to visit nor did he encourage visits, but from what I could gather, he seemed like a nice guy, and his wife, my Aunt Geri, seemed like a nice lady. It was only during the final few years of his life that he and I began to have some contact—by phone and by letter—about our mutual interest in family history.

This photo of my Uncle Jack was taken either while he was home on leave during the war, or shortly after it was over.

Uncle Jack and the U-Boat

One result of our long period of mutual indifference (I really don't know what else to call it) is that I did not realize until shortly before his death in 2001 that Uncle Jack had served in the Coast Guard during World War II, and also in the Army during the Korean War. Apparently, there were a number of times during his first term of service when he and his shipmates had some sort of close encounter with the enemy, but I think that the most interesting one I learned about was his participation in the capture, toward the end of World War II, of a German U-Boat, its captain, and its entire crew!

I'm sure its common knowledge that during both the First and Second World Wars, Germany used a fleet of U-boats to sink not only military vessels but also merchant ships. (By the way, in case you didn't know, the "U" in "U-boat" is short for "unter." The entire German word for this type of vessel is actually *unterseeboot*, literally "undersea boat," or as we say in the English-speaking world, *submarine*.) What seems not to be common knowledge, although apparently it was at the time, is that during World War II, these U-boats often made it all the way across the Atlantic, where they prowled the coasts of the United States, trying, and oftentimes succeeding, in sinking American ships bound for Europe. They also operated in the Gulf of Mexico.

In one notorious episode, which occurred in the summer of 1942, a German U-Boat actually surfaced at night, undetected, just off the coast of New York's Long Island, to allow four Gestapo-trained saboteurs to go ashore. This incident, largely forgotten today, was recently reenacted in the PBS Masterpiece Series, "Atlantic Crossing." Four more were dropped off, in a similar fashion, on a Florida beach by a different U-boat.

Although the Long Island group managed to get ashore and make their way to New York City—after burying explosives in the sand at the beach where they arrived—the saboteurs were soon discovered and taken into custody by the FBI. Before their trial, where a verdict of guilty was handed down, two of the eight Nazis cooperated with the government. Consequently, they received life sentences, whereas the other six were executed by electrocution.

Earlier that same year (1942), two American ships had been sunk by German submarines near the coast of the United States, one only 75 miles from New York City and the other only 60 miles from Long Island. U-boats were also notoriously active off the coast of North Carolina and in the Gulf of Mexico.

So, how did my Uncle Jack get involved in the capture of one of these nefarious U-boats? Well, it all started when the Japanese Navy attacked Pearl Harbor on December 7, 1941 and the United States officially declared war on Japan the following day (with Nazi Germany and Fascist Italy declaring war on the U.S. only days later). At the time, Uncle Jack was nineteen years old and working as a Western

Union messenger in downtown Dallas, Texas. He was also, despite his tender age, a married man. He and his wife, the former Geraldine Sheba Sharpe, had wed the previous June (1940), when Jack was seventeen and Geri only fourteen! Amazingly, considering how young they both were at the time, Uncle Jack and his bride were still happily married when Aunt Geri died fifty-eight years later, in 1998.

Jack began his service in the United States Coast Guard in early 1942. Following a two-month-long training course at Chicago, Illinois, he came home on ten-day's leave in April. A brief notice in the *Dallas Morning News* said that Aunt Geri would be joining him at his next duty station. Unfortunately, I don't know where that was, nor am I certain what he was doing until November 1, 1943, when he was assigned to a newly-built Destroyer Escort called the *U.S.S. Vance*, and that's when the action began.

The following description and account of the *U.S.S. Vance* and its activities during World War II comes from an official U.S. Navy publication:

> *Vance* (DE-387) was laid down on 30 April 1943 at Houston, Tex., by the Brown Shipbuilding Co.; launched on 16 July 1943; sponsored by Mrs. John W. Vance, mother of the late Lt. (jg.) Vance; and commissioned on 1 November 1943, Lt. Comdr. E. A. Anderson, USCG, in command.
>
> Following shakedown off Bermuda, *Vance* became the flagship for Escort Division (CortDiv) 45, a Coast Guard-manned unit, and convoyed a group of oil tankers from Norfolk, Va., to Port Arthur, Tex., and back. Upon her return to Norfolk,

she served as a training ship for destroyer escort crews while awaiting the arrival of the rest of her division.

This official Navy photo of the *U.S.S. Vance* was taken more than twenty years after Uncle Jack last served aboard it.

In February 1944, the ship conducted local escort operations before joining the New York section of Convoy UGS-33, bound for Gibraltar. Her section rendezvoused off Norfolk with the remainder of the convoy and its flagship, *Bibb* (WPG-31), and set out across the Atlantic. On 7 March, *Vance* departed Casablanca with GUS-33 for the return voyage and put into the New York Navy Yard on the 23d for availability.

Vance next got underway on 12 April, with the other ships of CortDiv 45 and a Navy-manned destroyer escort division, to screen the 102 merchantmen of convoy UGS-39 to Tunisia. Arriving at Bizerte on 3 May, the warship left Tunisian waters eight days later, bound for New York with GUS-39. Off Oran on the 14th, a German U-boat slipped through the screen of escorts and torpedoed two merchantmen. *Vance,* holding the "whip" position of the screen (where she had the duty of shepherding stragglers) came up through the convoy, sighted the periscope, and attempted to ram. The U-boat "pulled the plug" and dove deeper, evading the onrushing escort's sharp bow.

Vance remained on the scene for 10 hours, subjecting the U-boat to depth-charge and hedgehog attacks, until relieved by a squadron of Navy destroyers. Three days later, after an extensive hunt, the relief ships sank *U-616.*

Altogether, *Vance* made eight round-trip voyages to the western Mediterranean and followed each with availability at either Boston or New York. Four times the ship engaged in training exercises out of Casco Bay, sharpening up her antisubmarine and gunnery skills. On 14 July 1944, *Vance* helped to fight off a German air attack against an Allied convoy off Oran. During most of the voyages, the destroyer escort held the "whip'" position in the convoy, a grueling and sometimes frustrating detail since merchantmen frequently displayed a lack of discipline and straggled behind the convoy. Carrying the division doctor on board, *Vance* on occasion would take on board men from other ships for medical treatment.

On 2 May 1945, *Vance* departed New York with her last Mediterranean-bound convoy. On the morning of 11 May, four days after Germany had surrendered, *Vance* sighted a light up ahead in the convoy and rang down full speed to investigate. Upon closing the light, the destroyer escort discovered a surfaced U-boat, *U-873,* which had been at sea for 50 days. While the submarine began to run, *Vance* hailed the erstwhile enemy in German by bullhorn, ordering the submariners to heave to. *Vance* placed a prize crew on board the captured U-boat who delivered the prize at Portsmouth, N.H., on the 16th.[1]

---

[1] James L. Mooney, Ed., *Dictionary of American Naval Fighting ships, Volume VII* (Washington, D.C.: Naval Historical Center, United States Navy, 1981), 455.

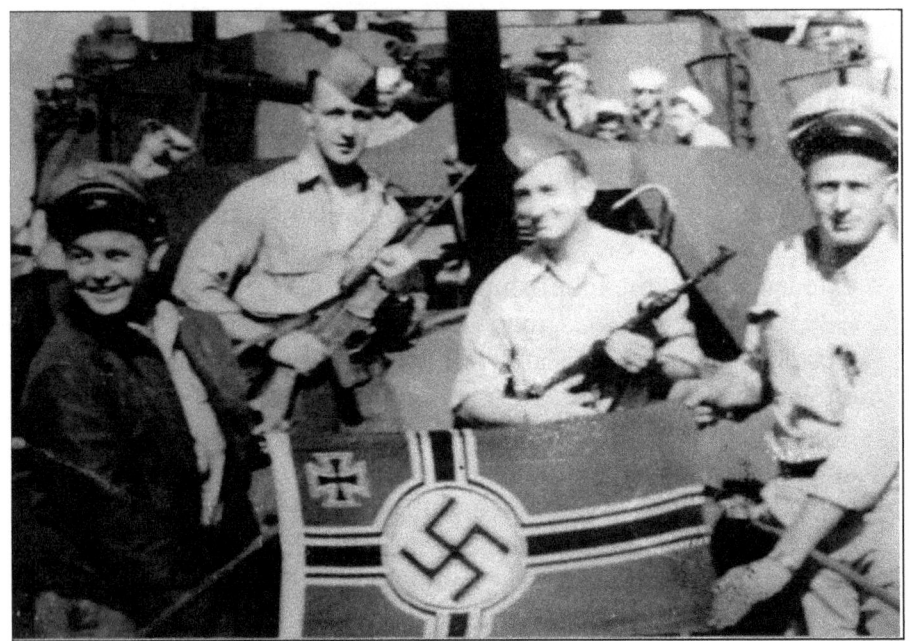

Jack Jenkins, left, with shipmates and captured German U-Boat flag.

Following the capture of the 1,200-ton *U-873*, its crew—48 enlisted men and 11 officers—were taken under guard aboard the *Vance*. A photo of Uncle Jack, smiling and helping a shipmate hold up the German vessel's flag, replete with Nazi swastika, while other *Vance* crew members pose with captured German weapons, provides proof that the American sailors helped themselves to war trophies while they could.

Commander T. Kincaid Kimmel, in charge of the prize crew that brought the U-boat from its point of capture to a mooring on the Piscataqua River in Portsmouth, New Hampshire, described the submarine as "very well-built" with "excellent guns," but "filthy," adding that it was well-stocked with food and supplies. "We found cans of food tucked into every nook and cranny of it," he said, "and plenty of beer, cognac and champagne." The crew was described as "dirty" and "pretty poor specimens of a master race."[2]

At Portsmouth, the U-boat sailors were taken off the *Vance* and immediately incarcerated. Their captain, Fritz Steinhoff, said one American officer, "was the toughest, most arrogant of all the prisoners captured. His only statement in response to many questions was, 'I am a Nazi, I will always be a Nazi.'" After he and his men were transferred to the Charles Street Jail in Boston, where they underwent interrogation, Steinhoff slashed his wrists with broken glass from a pair of sunglasses rather than divulge any information. After he was found bleeding in his cell, he was rushed by ambulance to Massachusetts General Hospital but died enroute. At the time of his death, Steinhoff was thirty-five-years-old and had been in charge of the *U-873*—his second such command— since March 1, 1944. He was buried at the post cemetery in Fort Devens, Suffolk County, Massachusetts. Referring to his suicide, Lt. (jg) Elliot Winslow, who took the photo of Steinhoff seen on the following page, said: "He set a good example for more of his ilk to follow."[3]

---

[2] *The Boston Globe*, Boston, Massachusetts, May 17, 1945.
[3] United States Coast Guard Historian's Office, Argo, WPC-100 [https://www.history.uscg.mil/US-

Kapitänleutnant Friedrich or Fritz Steinhoff, captain of the U-873 photo courtesy the Winslow family and the U.S. Coast Guard's Historian's Office.

Enlisted members of the *U-873's* crew were apparently more cooperative. The boat's home base, it was learned, was Kiel, but it had left from the port of Trondheim, Norway forty-seven days before the *Vance* found it. They said they had sunk a ship off Newfoundland before their capture. Of the sub's twenty-one torpedoes, six had been fired. The *U-873* was a new boat, having been launched on November 11, 1943, which made it almost exactly the same age as the

Coast-Guard-Photo-Gallery/igphoto/2002283256/; accessed 24 March 2021].

Vance. Its most interesting feature was a "schnorchel," a recently-invented device that allowed diesel-powered submarines to operate underwater without using their batteries. A year after the war, the boat was sold for scrap. In the meantime, the *Vance*:

> ...underwent alterations to her antiaircraft armament and soon got underway for the Pacific. However, she arrived too late to participate in anything but training operations and returned to the east coast for decommissioning. In mid-October 1945, she underwent a pre-deactivation availability before proceeding south to Green Cove Springs, Fla. On 27 February 1946, *Vance* was decommissioned and placed in reserve.[4]

****

After he left the service, sometime in 1945 or '46, Uncle Jack returned to civilian life and started to raise a family. A daughter had been born during the war and two more—my cousins—came along afterward.

One of my biggest regrets is that after I got in touch with Uncle Jack later on in both our lives, I didn't take the time to record an interview with him about his and my mother's family and just as importantly, his military service during World War II. If I had done that, this chapter might have been longer! But I didn't, and by the time it occurred to me, it was too late. Uncle Jack died at the age of seventy-nine

---

[4] Mooney, 455.

on July 25, 2001 and was afterward entombed in a mausoleum in Arlington, Texas, not far from the home in nearby Grand Prairie that he had shared with Aunt Geri for decades.

So, let that be a lesson to any family historians who may be reading this book: Don't procrastinate! If you have an elderly relative who might be able to provide valuable information about your family tree, ask them to consent to an interview and if they do, make sure you record it, either on audio, or better yet, make a video recording. If you don't, you may end up regretting it, as I have.

The "Old Salt" and His Stories

Uncle Jack, whose World War II experiences I wrote about in the previous chapter, was the oldest of my mother's two brothers, both of who were older than her. The other was my Uncle Lindell Ray Jenkins, a merchant seaman who after he retired in 1969, became legendary among family, friends and acquaintances for his bountiful repertoire of seemingly implausible tales. Most of his stories fell into one of two categories. They were either about famous people he said he met at various times in his life *a la Forrest Gump*—individuals whose careers he allegedly shaped with his advice—or they centered on ideas that were supposedly taken from him (or in one case, his mother) and used by other people to make fortunes. Styling himself the "Old Salt," Lindell recorded these tales in a weekly newspaper column he wrote from 1982 until sometime in the late 1990s for a series of Houston-area publications—each of which was the free, give-away type commonly found on racks beside the front doors of laundromats and convenience stores. For nearly two decades, he unfailingly sent me copies of each and every one, and not just clippings but the entire paper, folded in every conceivable way so as to fit into an ordinary #10 envelope. He also sent copies to other family members, and probably to friends that didn't live in Houston, Texas, where he resided.

Because of his stories, and other reasons, I'm sure that most of his closest relatives considered Lindell, as I did, something of a "character"—a peculiar but harmless eccentric who had perhaps "spent a little too much time at sea," a suspicion seemingly confirmed in September 1968 when he was taken into custody by authorities at St. John's, Newfoundland, where he'd recently arrived aboard the *USNS Pecos*. He was picked up on shore because he was allegedly behaving "in a rather strange manner" and then judged by two psychiatrists to be in need of institutionalization. Lindell avoided that fate, however, because the Canadians agreed to release him to my stepfather, who flew all the way from Chicago to personally bring him back to the United States.

Among the behaviors that the Canadian authorities found odd was that Lindell, as they put it, seemed "restless" and also "overtalkative." They remarked as well that "he showed flight of ideas and expressed delusions of grandeur." If I had been there, I would have told them, "Hell, that's just Uncle Lindell being Uncle Lindell. That's normal for him." "Overtalkative" was certainly a good choice of words. Once Lindell got started, you could not get a word in edgewise. I have a video-recording of him talking non-stop for approximately 45 minutes on all manner of topics. Once, I tried to digitally edit it so that I could insert

The "Old Salt" and His Stories

explanatory frames between topics, but gave up the effort because there were no discernible pauses that made it possible. Once he got going, there was no stopping him until he was good and ready to stop.

Throughout his life, Lindell also exhibited signs of obsessive-compulsive disorder by doing on multiple occasions the exact same thing. For example, he was married five times. So what, you might say, surely he wasn't the only man who's been married five times? Yes, *but to the same woman*? The first time Lindell and Aunt Betsy got married was in 1944, the second in 1945, the third in 1947, the fourth in 1949, and the fifth in 1953. I do not know if they were officially divorced between each marriage because I've found a record of only one, in 1951. To the best of my knowledge, when Lindell died in 2000, he and my Aunt Betsy were still legally married, even though they had not lived together as husband and wife for decades.

Sometimes, when people get older, they exhibit signs of senile dementia combined with paranoia, but apparently, Lindell was doing that long before he reached old age. Many years ago, when I was an infant, he spent some days or weeks living with my parents and me in East Dallas. Now, I don't personally remember this, but years later, my dad told me that during Lindell's stay, from time-to-time he would get up from wherever he was sitting, go to the front of the house, carefully draw back the curtains, and then glance furtively out the window. When my dad asked him why he kept doing this, Lindell replied, "I think they are watching me," or words to that effect, without clarifying who "they" were. My dad said he reckoned one of two things: Either Lindell had either actually done something to attract the attention of authorities, or he was simply imagining things, *or was he*? My cousin Kathleen once told me that one time her father actually *was* being watched by the FBI because he had written a threatening letter to President Jimmy Carter. I've never seen the letter, but knowing Lindell, I can't think it was actually antagonistic. I *can* imagine, however, that it was strange enough to cause worry. In any event, said Kathleen, when a federal agent followed her father into the men's room of a bar or restaurant that Lindell frequented, my uncle, who had noticed the man (*who he didn't know was a federal agent*), looking at him earlier, thought he had come in there for some nefarious reason and, according to Kathleen, he slugged the guy. I've found no record of this incident in the press, so I have only Kathleen's word for it, but I don't doubt it's true.

My uncle was also an impulsive person. Another story my dad told me was that during the same time I mentioned earlier, while my then-young uncle was staying with us, he applied for and got a job at some business in or near downtown Dallas, where my dad's workplace was also located. On the morning that Lindell was supposed to start his new job, he walked with my dad to the nearest bus stop, so that they could ride the bus into town together. However, before the bus arrived, my dad said that Lindell suddenly told him that he didn't want the job after all and as he started to walk off by himself down the sidewalk, yelled back that he was going to go to Houston instead, to see if he could sign aboard some merchant ship there, and apparently, that's just what he did.

I can personally attest to Lindell's impulsive nature. Just after Christmas in 1998, he invited me to go with him and his daughter—my cousin Kathleen—in his car to Muskogee, Oklahoma, where he wanted to put some paving bricks he'd found somewhere around a small grave marker that he had earlier placed in Frozen Rock Cemetery. That's the spot where Lindell's mother—my grandmother, and Kathleen's—was buried after she died of tuberculosis, at age thirty, in 1934. Here we have another example of Lindell's OCD. The marker that he wished to embellish with a circle of bricks was but the most recent of three that my uncle placed there in the decade before he died. It's unlikely, however, that any of the three marked the actual spot where our grandmother was buried since no one, not even Lindell, who had gone to the funeral (but was only a kid at the time), could remember exactly where the originally unmarked grave was located.

In any event, upon arrival in Muskogee well after noon, Kathleen and I begged Uncle Lindell to stop at an El Chico Mexican Restaurant so that we could have some lunch before going out to the cemetery, which is located on the eastern outskirts of town. After he begrudgingly agreed and we were parked in the restaurant parking lot, he asked me to help him check the oil in his car, which was an old one that had been given or loaned to him by Uncle Jack. When I said the dipstick indicated that he probably needed a couple of quarts, he closed the hood of the car and then we all three started for the front entrance of the restaurant, *or so I thought*. When Kathleen and I entered the front door, without looking back I held it open for Uncle Lindell, *but soon realized he wasn't coming up behind us*! Where had he gone? We looked to see if the car was still there in the parking lot. It was. *But where was Lindell?*

To make a long story short, Kathleen and I shrugged our shoulders and went inside, got a table and started looking at menus while waiting for her father to show up. Two or three times we told the waiter to come back when he came over to take our order. Eventually, we decided to go ahead and by the time Uncle Lindell finally arrived, Kathleen and I were nearly finished eating our enchiladas! "Where did you go Uncle Lindell? I asked him. "I went to get oil," he replied. Apparently, he could not wait until after lunch to buy oil, so while Kathleen and I were headed to the front door of the restaurant, he was off on a mission, striding down the sidewalk to an auto parts store some two or three blocks away! Then, after buying two or three cans of motor oil, he came striding back and proceeded to empty it into the car while my cousin and I were enjoying our lunch. Naturally, Kathleen and I were a little taken aback, and annoyed, but what could we do? *That was Uncle Lindell!*

Yes, there's no doubt that my Uncle Lindell was a one-of-a-kind person. Here's one more example: In 1976, seven years after he made his last voyage as an Able Seaman on a ship called the *S.S. Gulf Deer*, he decided to go into politics, but instead of running for city council or some state or federal office as a candidate for one of the two major parties, instead he went for the big time, or rather, he tried. Yes, you probably guessed it. He decided to run for President of the United States as the nominee of the "Commonwealth Political Party of the United States of America," of which I think he was probably the only member. What was its platform? Answer: I don't know, because Lindell wasn't too clear about that. He *did* get his name in the newspaper though, in West Virginia, where a reporter mistook his given name for a female name saying that Lindell didn't get on the ballot in that state because "she" hadn't paid the required filing fee. He tried again in 1988 and as before, got a little press—in Mississippi and North Carolina—but also as before, paid no filing fee and therefore wasn't on the ballot that year either. I heard from someone (probably my cousin, Kathleen) that he had put my stepfather's name down as his Vice-Presidential running mate (apparently without either his knowledge or consent), but I can't confirm that.

My Uncle Lindell Jenkins in a photo that was used for some of the headers of his "Old Salt" newspaper columns in the 1990s.

The "Old Salt" and His Stories

Uncle Lindell's generosity bears mentioning, although the gifts he gave were rarely something you'd want or need. When I was a toddler, he gave me a baby duckling for Easter, but I had nowhere to keep it after it was grown, so my parents gave it to my mother's aunt and uncle, who kept chickens and geese in their backyard in East Dallas. Much later, he gave me a pair of sneakers and then a pair of cowboy boots. In both instances it wasn't my birthday nor was it Christmas. It was just something he did on the spur-of-the-moment. So, you may ask, what's wrong with that? Nothing, if either the shoes or the boots were my size or my taste, but they weren't. Unfortunately, he never asked me what size shoe or boot I wore, or even if I'd like a pair of boots. He just sent them. In the end, I gave the shoes to charity and the boots too, after I wore them one time—to his funeral—although they were too tight. I felt it was the least I could do. After all, he meant well.

When I was in junior high school, Uncle Lindell *did* send me something I liked—a black beret from Lisbon, Portugal, a port he probably visited while serving on either the *SS Ruth Lykes* or the *SS Virginia Lykes*. This was in the early '60s. In this case, the item fit and his timing couldn't have been better. At that time, I was fascinated by beatniks. The black beret was perfect attire when my friends and I opened a short-lived beatnik coffee shop in my family's garage, in a small town where actual beatniks were as scarce as hen's teeth. I also wore it when I went to church camp that summer, so much so that the other kids nicknamed me "Frenchie," even though the beret was clearly marked "Made in Portugal," not France.

Nearly every summer during the last decade-and-a-half of his life, Uncle Lindell also sent me a hurricane tracking chart that he probably picked up for free at some Houston drugstore. If I had lived near the coast, like him, it might have been useful, but I didn't and therefore it wasn't. I guess he imagined we had hurricanes in North Central Texas too. He also sent free drugstore calendars from time-to-time, which actually were quite useful.

One year, for Christmas, I sent him a large belt buckle with the state seal of Oklahoma on it. I thought he would like it since he was born in Oklahoma. As it turned out, he liked it very much, and in return, he sent me a similar buckle, but with the Texas state seal on it. It wasn't the sort of thing I'd wear, unfortunately, and I never did. I still have it in the box in which he sent it, but as it's often said, it's the thought that counts.

In more or less the same vein, in 1991 Lindell also arranged for Bill Clements, the then-Governor of Texas, to issue a certificate making me an honorary "Admiral" of the non-existent "Texas Navy," which was likewise a nice thoughtful gesture, except that whoever typed my name on the certificate misspelled my first name, but that was hardly the first time that's happened.

The "Old Salt" and His Stories

Lindell Ray Jenkins in 1943, shortly after joining the U.S. Maritime Service.

One gift from Lindell that I definitely had no use for was a big box of Bibles. Why he sent them, I don't know, and I never asked, but there must have been twenty or thirty of them in the box. However, as I've pointed out already, my uncle seemed to like multiples of things. I ended up giving them to my father's church since I had no plans to open one of my own! This gift was odd too because up to that time I had never heard Uncle Lindell say anything at all about religion, never heard him pray, or anything. To this day, I have no idea what his religious views were, or if he went to church regularly, or anything at all like that. He never brought it up, so I don't think it's something in which he had any great interest.

Another thing Lindell did in multiples was join veterans' organizations. After retiring, he became a member of the American Merchant Marine Veterans, the American Legion, Disabled American Veterans (although he was not himself disabled, at least not in any way I could discern), AMVETS, the Veterans of Foreign Wars, and the National Maritime Union (NMU), for which he worked in the Houston area as a sort of "gopher" when he was not busy traveling around the country, visiting relatives (most frequently my mother or his daughter, Kathleen) or when he was writing up his "Old Salt" stories.

Lindell also spent some time during his retirement years seeking recognition for his twenty-six years of service aboard no fewer than eighty-two different vessels—a period that encompassed World War II, the Korean War, and the War in Vietnam. He was especially proud of a medal that the Russian government awarded him and other American merchant seamen for their contribution to the Soviet Union's victory over Nazi Germany during World War II.

And now, the "Old Salt's" stories!

In tacit recognition of Lindell's eccentric personality and also out of consideration for his sensitivities, no one in the family, to the best of my knowledge, ever challenged the

The "Old Salt" and His Stories

veracity of his tall tales. When telling these stories, he always did so with a straight face and never gave any indication that he might be trying to pull your leg. To this very day, I wonder if there was a time in his life when he *knew* these stories to be the fabrications that they surely were, but, having told them for so long and so often, he ultimately reached a point where he was no longer able to distinguish between fact and fiction in his own mind.

Although I usually took these stories with a grain of salt, for a while after Lindell died, I entertained the notion that these stories, or perhaps some of them, might contain at least some small grain of truth. One reason for my willingness to accept this possibility is the lack of variation in these tales. Regardless of his audience, Uncle Lindell was generally consistent, telling the same story more or less the same way every time. Another thing that struck me was how specific some of the details were. Eventually, I decided to try to find out if there could be anything to them. And so, dear reader, here, for your entertainment and edification, are some of the "Old Salt's" best-known and most frequently told tales, followed by the results of my investigation.

The MARGARET MITCHELL
(Author of "Gone with the Wind") Story

The last time I heard this story was when I accompanied my uncle on a "nostalgia trip" to his native Muskogee, Oklahoma a little less than two years before he died: In the early 1930s, before his mother died and when he was still in elementary school, Lindell supposedly earned money by selling newspapers at the Muskogee train station to departing passengers. One day, a lady was sitting on a bench on the platform, holding some sheets of paper that she was either reading, writing on, or correcting with a pen or pencil. Suddenly, a gust of wind came along and blew some of the pages out of her hands. Being a gallant young lad, my uncle put down his newspapers (presumably he first secured them with something heavy, to prevent them from also blowing away), leapt down from the platform, and chased the errant sheets down the railroad track. After recovering each and every one, he presented them to the astonished but grateful woman, who just happened to be the not-yet-famous Georgia author, Margaret Mitchell. "Here you go lady," he told her as he handed them back, "I thought these were gone with the wind!" *And indeed, they were*, since the flyaway sheets of paper that Mitchell was sitting there working on, were pages from her forthcoming novel! The implication was that without realizing it at the time, Lindell had provided Ms. Mitchell with a title for her epic work, which she was then struggling to come up with.

So, did my Uncle Lindell inadvertently help Margaret Mitchell decide on a title for her best-selling book? Although Mitchell *was* working on her novel during this period, it seems unlikely. Obviously, the only way to learn whether or not this story could possibly be true is to try to find out if Margaret Mitchell was ever in Muskogee prior to 1934, when, following the death of this mother, Lindell and his father and siblings moved to Dallas, Texas. Long story short: So far as I know, she wasn't.

There's also the fact that in 1936, shortly after *Gone with the Wind* was published, Mitchell was asked how she chose the title of her book. She admitted it hadn't been easy—some of the titles she considered were *Tomorrow is Another Day*, or *There's Always Tomorrow*, which are variations of a line spoken in the book (and also the movie) by the character, Scarlett "O'Hara, but one thing is certain: When asked about the title, she never said anything about a paper boy in Muskogee, Oklahoma giving her the idea for it!

So, was Uncle Lindell pulling our leg about this one? It certainly seems so.

The AUDIE MURPHY
(most decorated soldier of World War II) Story

This celebrated war hero of World War II figured prominently in one of Uncle Lindell's most frequently related adventures. Around 1942, when he was seventeen and living in Dallas, my uncle and a friend J. L. Hall, "who was a Cherokee" Indian, said Lindell, went to visit Hall's grandmother "in a small [East Texas] community with a cotton gin." At that time, the two friends had been considering enlisting in the army together. For one reason or another, Lindell decided not to spend the night, but to hitchhike back to Dallas. (How the two youths reached their destination in the first place is something my uncle failed to mention.) "As I walked up toward the town, across from the cotton gin," Lindell recalled many years later, "I saw a man standing against a post" outside a little café. When my uncle asked him how to get to the highway leading to Dallas, he was told "go straight down the road a few miles." After the man called Lindell's attention to the fact that it was almost dark, he replied optimistically that he would probably get a ride before he reached the highway. Expressing doubt, the man explained that he was waiting for his wife to finish cleaning up the café, which was about to close. After telling Lindell to wait, he went inside and conferred with his spouse. When he emerged, he told my uncle that as soon as his wife was through with her chores, they could drive him as far as Farmersville. From there, he could take a bus back to Dallas. Inviting him inside, the man's wife, said Lindell, "placed a big bowl of chili in front of me, which I ate and thanked her for."

When he was finished eating, Lindell joined the café-owner on the porch. By this time, it was dark outside. Suddenly, my uncle saw another young man emerge from the shadow of the cotton gin. As he walked toward the café, the man who had befriended my uncle called out, "Hello Audie."

After returning the man's greeting, the youth addressed my uncle. "I have been looking for you," said Audie Murphy (whom Lindell had presumably never met until that night). "You have?" replied Lindell. "Yes, J. L. Hall told me that you and he planned to volunteer for the army." When my uncle replied in the affirmative, Murphy told him he also hoped to enlist. At this, the older man interrupted. "Who is going to take care of your mother and sisters? You are the oldest son and you work for me sometimes." "That's true," Murphy allegedly replied, "but if I am in the army, they will send them money." Lindell recalled that soldiers got paid about $21 a month, "a big sum for those days."

As they conversed, Murphy supposedly said: "You know those people [the Germans and the Japanese] shoot to kill. You and I have never shot anything but rabbits for food." Lindell claimed to have replied: "You have to treat them like your enemy and shoot back to kill them, but that's what you call going to hell and back. (I've always thought it was interesting how in the middle of this story, Uncle Lindell managed to work in the title of Murphy's postwar memoirs and box office hit movie.)

Instead of taking Lindell to Farmersville, the café-owner and his wife agreed to drive both Lindell and Audie Murphy in their pick-up truck to Dallas. "I told them that I lived near the fairgrounds where the rides were," my uncle later recalled (at least that much was true), "so Audie and I rode in the back of the pick-up truck to Dallas and I went home to ask my dad to sign papers for me to go in the army."

Lindell did not say whether Audie Murphy accompanied him to his home in South Dallas, near the fairgrounds, but he did conclude the story by stating that his father refused to give his permission for him to join the army. Murphy, who was supposedly already eighteen at the time, needed no such permission. Apparently, Lindell's soldierly ambitions were fleeting. In the summer of 1943, after he turned eighteen, he enlisted in the United States Maritime Service instead.

So, did Uncle Lindell really meet Audie Murphy on his way to enlist in the army? Let's see. Lindell *did* live in Dallas in those days and Murphy *did* live near Farmersville, in nearby Hunt County, but then so did a lot of other people live in those two places at that time, so that proves nothing.

Let's look also at the supposed age difference: As it happens Audie Murphy and Lindell Jenkins were both born in June 1925, Murphy on the 20th and Lindell on the 26th, so there was really no discernable difference in their ages. However, Murphy enlisted on June 30, 1942, when he was only seventeen, it's said by falsifying his age, which Lindell could have done too if he really wanted to join the army badly.

Perhaps the best reason we can be sure this story isn't true is because if it took place in the month and year that Audie Murphy enlisted, that is June 1942, it's not likely that

Lindell was hitchhiking to East Texas or anywhere else. Why? Because on May 29, 1942, about a month before Audie Murphy enlisted in the Army, Lindell and three other young men were indicted by a Tarrant County, Texas grand jury for robbing taxi drivers, after they were arrested and jailed in Dallas. The amounts were small, a few dollars here, a few dollars there. Moreover, the robberies were committed when Lindell was a juvenile, although he was an adult by the time he was tried. Unfortunately, the outcome of Lindell's trial seems to have been lost to history, but my Cousin Kathleen confided that as a result of his brief brush with the law, her dad spent some months in a Juvenile Detention facility. For that reason, it's a near certainty that while Audie Murphy was signing his enlistment papers, Lindell was cooling his heels in either the Dallas or the Tarrant County Jail, to which he and the three other young men were transferred after being picked up in Dallas.

The ELVIS PRESLEY (King of Rock 'n' Roll) Story
According to Lindell, singer Elvis Presley was a distant relative to whom he once gave some important career advice. As my uncle told it, after his grandfather, William Newton Jenkins died in September 1946, he and his father, Ollie, traveled to Mississippi to bring his aunt, Lena Morrison (William Newton Jenkins' adopted daughter), back to Dallas to attend the funeral. At that time, Lena, a deaf-mute, was living with some distant cousins, Della and

Arthur Morrison, on their home near Tupelo. After a long and no doubt tiring drive, Lindell and his father arrived there late at night.

The following morning, while Della was cooking breakfast, Lindell's father asked him to go to the back door of the house and call Arthur, who was out plowing a field. "I walked to the back door," Lindell later recalled, "and hollered breakfast was ready and came back." When Arthur failed to appear, Della told him to go back to the door and yell, "The biscuits is ready!" Lindell complied and apparently these words got the older man's attention because he stopped plowing. As Lindell watched from the back door of the farmhouse, he "saw a boy taking the reins [from Arthur], to put behind his head, to plow behind the horse."

After breakfast, Lindell noticed a guitar hanging on a wall of the house. Having nothing better to do, he took it down and started strumming it. A few minutes later, recalled Lindell, "the door opened and it was that boy I thought was still plowing." The young man's name, as it turned out, was Elvis Presley.[1] "He said I was holding the guitar wrong and [that] it was his." When Elvis supposedly told him "that sometimes people would ask him to play for them" Lindell advised the boy to make a recording. He explained how servicemen "made records and sent them home to their

---

[1] At this time, Elvis was about twelve years old.

families and friends." Lindell also told Elvis "how a...brother-in-law, Walter Strow II, made his [own records] and played them at [the] WRR...radio station in Dallas."

Lindell added that before they left Mississippi, he and Ollie saw Elvis and his father Vernon at a general store owned by another Morrison relative. When Lindell overheard the youngster asking for a new pair of shoes that Vernon couldn't afford, he suggested that his storeowner relative let the Presleys "sign" for the shoes, i.e., buy them on credit. "Elvis got his shoes," Lindell said and later recalled that Elvis allegedly told him "that he had been thinking about what I had told him about making his own records." Lindell encouraged the boy to come to Dallas where he promised to "show him how to make them and take them to a radio station to get them" played on the air. "In those days," Lindell claimed, "it was easy to get a radio station to play a record if it was a good one."

Although Vernon Presley was broke, or nearly so, said Lindell, he had other plans. He wanted to take his family to live in Memphis, Tennessee. Lindell recalled that a "loan" of seventeen dollars from his father, Ollie Jenkins, helped pave their way. Before they parted company, Elvis asked Lindell "what he should write about in his songs." He told him "to write about his sweet mama and make his own records." Lindell also advised him "to move around to get people's attention" when he sang his songs.

Could this story be true? *Let's see.* Though the Presleys didn't move to Memphis until 1948, rather than 1946, as Lindell said, we could dismiss this error as the result of faulty memory. Or maybe Elvis' daddy used the seventeen dollars for something else? What strikes me is how Lindell was so specific about the amount of money his father allegedly loaned Vernon Presley—not just "some money" but *"seventeen dollars."* Unfortunately, there's one facet of the story that we can't so easily dismiss. Although the Vernon Presley family, who were poor sharecroppers, *did* live in or near Tupelo, Mississippi around this time, Della and Arthur Morrison—who were also real people by the way—lived on a farm more than 200 miles away, near Utica, Mississippi.

There's also a problem with the obituary of William Newton Jenkins stating that Lena then lived at Leonard, Mississippi, a place that apparently no longer exists, so it's impossible to say where it was in relation to either Utica or Tupelo, but it's certainly not either one. The published "Old Salt" stories about this incident indicates it took place at Tupelo. In the margin of a clipping of at least one version, all of which are similar, Lindell wrote that it actually occurred at Utica, Mississippi, which puts Uncle Arthur and Aunt Della in the right place, but not Elvis's family.

What I also find doubtful is that Lindell and his father drove all the way to Mississippi for the purpose of bringing Lena back to Dallas for her adopted father's funeral. Since there were no interstate highways at the time, the trip would probably have taken at least four days or more. More likely, they drove there *after* the funeral and brought her back to live with Lindell's Aunt Pearl and her husband Earnest Hayes. I do know that she lived with them in the 1950s and 1960s because I saw her there with my own eyes when I was a child.

Bottom line: *What we have here is another whopper!*

The HANK WILLIAMS
(Country & Western Music Legend) Story

Lindell claimed that while he was serving aboard the tugboat *Toddie L.* in 1945, an inter-coastal vessel that traveled regularly between Carabelle, Florida and Corpus Christi, Texas, one of his shipmates was none other than legendary Country and Western musician Hiram or "Hank" Williams, with whom he allegedly collaborated on several songs.

The *Toddie L.*, recalled Lindell, was owned by the American Liberty Oil Company and named for Toddie L. Wynn of Dallas. The captain's name was Gus. One time, during a storm, my uncle remembered, "we were caught between the railroad bridge and the Galveston Island Causeway." While he was lashed with a rope to the top mast, said Lindell, "Hank Williams, Sr. would hand me the carbon stick that went into the search lights." The *Toddie L.*, he also alleged, "was the same boat we were on together…where the songs "Your Cheatin' Heart" and others came from." Williams, explained Lindell, "would turn off the switch where I wouldn't get electrocuted while putting in the carbide lights." They later went to Galveston, said my uncle, "where I shipped out on a tanker and where I turned down fifty dollars…to write songs for another man that we met in Galveston," a man that for some reason Williams didn't like.

Lindell also claimed that the boat's cook, a man named Mack, was a friend of Williams and that he (Lindell) got the idea for the song "Hey, Good Looking" from some place, probably a drinking establishment, where the men went to relax and socialize when they were not working aboard ship.

Could this story be true? In this case, the answer is an unequivocal "no." Although it is a fact that during World War II, Hank Williams, Sr. worked in a Mobile, Alabama shipyard before launching his musical career in 1946, there's no evidence that he ever served in the Merchant Marine. Perhaps he helped build the *Toddie L.* (and I'm not saying he did) but it's a near certainty he never served aboard it. There's no question about it: This one is a complete flight of fantasy.

The COLONEL SANDERS
(Fried Chicken purveyor) Story

Among Lindell's papers that I have in my possession is a hand-scrawled, undated letter addressed "To Whom It

The "Old Salt" and His Stories

May Concern," attesting to the truthfulness of this supposedly true story. Here it is.

"I have always been interested in my roots," wrote Lindell in his "Old Salt" column of August 17, 1984, "and on a trip to Georgia, I met Col. Harlan Sanders' nephew at a truck and bus stop." (Lindell didn't, unfortunately, say just when or in what town this occurred.) "We went on to his uncle's restaurant for supper." As the two men were eating, wrote Lindell, "a traveling salesman came in and ordered fried chicken and [said he] was in a hurry." Colonel Sanders allegedly told the salesman it would take too long to prepare fried chicken so he ordered a steak instead. At this point, Lindell commented that his mother used to cook chicken in a pressure cooker.

In the story, Lindell went on to say that he was invited to spend the night at the Colonel's home and the next day, showed him how to prepared fried chicken in a pressure cooker, the way his mother, Ida Lee Seay Jenkins, had done it in Muskogee. "I also [gave] him mother's secret recipe for seasoning it," added Lindell.

"I tasted the finished product," Lindell wrote, "and said, 'yes, this is Oklahoma fried chicken and it's finger lickin' good.'" The Colonel supposedly replied, "This is Kentucky and it's Kentucky Fried Chicken, and it really is finger lickin' good."

Obviously, there is a glaring discrepancy in this story. At the beginning, Lindell says he was in Georgia but at the end of the story, somehow, he is magically in Kentucky! In the hand-written affidavit referred to above, he wrote that the incident occurred "many years ago in Corbin, Kentucky." It's possible, perhaps, that Georgia was a typographical error or perhaps Lindell meant to say that he met the nephew in Georgia and they traveled to Kentucky together.

In any event, could this story be true? Well, our family does have roots in both Kentucky and Georgia, so it's possible that Lindell could have traveled to either place. Furthermore, Colonel Sanders did have a restaurant in Corbin, Kentucky at one time, but did he and Lindell meet there? And what about the recipe?

As I expected when I checked out this story, the official Kentucky Fried Chicken corporate history of Harlan Sanders and his "secret" recipe says nothing at all about the "Colonel" (an honorary title bestowed by the Governor of Kentucky) being taught how to cook chicken by a merchant sailor from Oklahoma. What it *does* say is that while operating a gas station in Corbin, Kentucky, the Colonel (who was actually from Indiana), began cooking up meals for travelers, serving them in his own living quarters. Eventually, he opened a motel and a restaurant across the street from the gas station. Over the next several years, he personally developed the special recipe that KFC still uses today. This was during the 1930s, by the way, when Lindell was just a school boy, growing up in Muskogee and later, in Dallas, Texas.

During the 1950s and early 1960s, when Lindell was most often at sea on some merchant vessel, Colonel Sanders, then in his sixties, was busy traveling throughout the United States, building the franchise chain that has since become a world-wide operation.

Bottom line: *Another whopper!*

****

There are lots of other well-known people that Uncle Lindell claimed to have had some sort of meaningful interaction during his life, including professional golfer Ben Hogan, who was supposedly a neighbor in Muskogee, Oklahoma. *He wasn't.* Hogan grew up in Fort Worth, Texas. Lindell also claimed that humorist Will Rogers and pilot Wiley Post visited the Jenkins family in Muskogee and that he saw Amie Semple McPherson preach there, which is a lot more likely than Will Rogers dropping by for a cup of coffee and a friendly chat. Other names Lindell mentioned in his "Old Salt" columns were Country singer Ernest Tubb, Secret Service Agent Melvin Cheney, actor Donald O'Connor, actor-singer Roy Rogers, musical performer Smiley Burnett, and Igor Sikorsky, who Lindell allegedly helped invent the helicopter, which of course seems unlikely for the simple reason that in 1909, when Sikorsky first designed a helicopter, Lindell hadn't yet been born! Uncle Lindell also claimed to have invented, or inspired someone else to build or invent, cellophane tape, parking meters, sliced bread, and the Astrodome in Houston.

One of my favorites in this line-up is Lindell's claim to have met music promoter Brian Epstein, while in port at Liverpool, England, where one night they purportedly sat together at the same table in the Cavern Club to watch a four-man rock n' roll band that Epstein was then managing perform. Uncle Lindell said that to him, the musicians, wearing black suits and wiggling around on stage, looked to him like a bunch of beetles, so he suggested that name to Epstein, who used it, except that he decided to spell it "Beatles" instead. Of course, this outrageous fabrication completely ignores the oft-told story of how the Beatles got their name, which was that they wanted an insect name, like Buddy Holly's "Crickets," so they decided on Beetles, but replaced the second "e" with an "a" in reference to the beat of the drums or to the so-called "beat" clubs in which they performed.

So, there you have it, dear reader, the straight scoop, so to speak, on my Uncle Lindell's tall tales and flights of fantasy, which might make you think, what a strange man! Yes, there's no doubt about that, but he was also a lot of fun, and I for one miss him.

Appendix I:

Text of Runaway Servant Ad placed by George Kastner in *Der Hoch-Deutsche Pensylvanische Geschicht-Schreiber,* offering a reward for the return of Conrad Wied (Conrad Wheat).

"George Kastner, in Whitpain Township, in Philadelphia County, makes known: that on June 17th last, a German Servant ran away, Named Conrad Wied about 30 years old, medium stature, brown thin spiky hair, fresh of face. His take-away clothing, is a red-brown Camisole, brown semi-linen pants, a good shirt of Work Cloth; a pair of shoes, full of Nails on the Soles, a Knap-Sack, a new shirt and long pants. His Camisole is lined with stripes of three or four different varieties; as well as a half-worn Felt-Cap, besides other things. Whoever reports Servant testifies and keeps, so, that his Master avoids embarrassment, should 50 Shillings have, besides reasonable expenses."

Appendix II:
Memorial to Congress for Erecting the Government of Westsylvania, 1776

To the Honorable the President and Delegates of the thirteen united American Colonies in General Congress assembled:

The Memorial of the Inhabitants of the Country, West of the Alleghany Mountains represents:

That - Whereas the Provinces of Pennsylvania & Virginia set up Claims to this large and extensive Country, which for a considerable comitants & pernicious & destructive Effects of discordant & contending Jurisdictions, innumerable Frauds, Impositions, Violences, Depredations, Feuds, Animosities, Divisions, Litigations, Disorders & even with the Effusion of human Blood, to the utter Subversion of all Laws human & divine of Justice, Order, Regularity & in a great Measure even of Liberty itself & must unless a timely speedy Stop be put to them in all Probability terminate in a Civil War, which how far it may effect the Union of the Colonies & the General Cause of America, we lean to your prudent, impartial & Serious Consideration.

And Whereas (exclusive of & as an Addition & further aggregation to the many accumulated Injuries & Miseries and complicated & insupportable Grievances & Oppressions, we already labor under, in Consequences of the aforesaid Claims & the Controversies, etc. thereby occasioned the fallacies, Violences, and fraudulent Impositions of Land Jobbers, Officers & Partisans of both Land Officers & others under the Sanction of the Jurisdiction of their respective Provinces, the Earl of Dunmore's Warrants, Officer's & Soldier's Rights & an Infinity of other Pretexts, in which they have of late proceeded so far, as in express Contradiction to the Declaration of the Continental Commissioners made on the ninth day of October 1775 at the Treaty of Fort Pitt made encroachments on the Indian

Territorial Rights by improving laying Warrants & Officers Claims & Surveying some of the Islands in the Ohio and Tomahawking (or as they term it) imposing in a Variety of Places on the Western side of the said River, to the great, imminent & Manifest Danger of the involving if the Country in a bloody, ruinous & destructive War with the Indians, a people extremely watchful, tenacious & jealous of their Rights, Privileges & Liberties, and already it is to be doubted, too much inclined to a Rupture and Commencement of Hostilities from the Persuasions & Influences of British Emissaries, Agents & Officers & the little attention unfortunately hitherto paid to them by the American Confederacy in Conciliating their affections, Confidence and Friendship:) there are a number of private or other Claims to Lands within the Limits of this Country, equally embarrassing & perplexing: George Croghan Esquire, in various Tracts, Claims Land by Purchase from the Six Nations in 1748 & confirmed to him at the Treaty of Fort Stanwix in 1768 to the Amount by Computation of 200,000 Acres on which are settled already 150 or 200 Families: Major William Trent in Behalf of himself & the Traders who suffered by the Indian Depredations in 1763 another large Tract containing at least 4,000,000 of Acres by Donation & Cession of the six Nations aforesaid at the aforesaid Treaty of Fort Stanwix in 1768 & on which 1,500 or 2,000 Families are already Settled: and there was on the 4th day of January 1770 a Certain Contract & Purchase made by the Honorable Thomas Walpole & Associates (including the Ohio Company & the Officers & Soldiers in the Service of the Colony of Virginia Claiming under the Engagements of that Colony in the year 1754) under the name of the Grand Ohio or Vandalia Company with & of the Lords Commissioners of the Treasury on Behalf of Crown for an Extensive Tract of Country within the Purchase & Cession from the aforesaid Six Nations & their Confederates at the said Treaty of Fort Stanwix aforesaid made & by his Majesty's Special Command & Direction notified to the Indians of the Western Tribes of the aforesaid Confederacy on the 3rd day of April 1773, by Alexander McKee, Esq. Deputy Agent of the Western Department for Indian Affairs on the claims of Scioto, who by their Answer of the 6th of the Same Month expressed their Approbation thereof, & Satisfaction & Acquiescence therein, at the same time justly observing that for the Peace of the Country it was as necessary for Prudent People to govern White Settlers as for the Indians to take Care of their foolish young men. This is a country of at least 240 Miles in Length from the Kittanning to opposite the mouth of Scioto 70 or 80 in Breadth from the Alleghany Mountains to the Ohio, rich, fertile & healthy even beyond a credibility & peopled by at least 25,000 Families since the year 1768 (a population we believe scarce to be paralleled in the Annals of any Country. Miserably distressed & harassed & rendered a scene of the most consumate Anarchy & Confusion by the Ambition of some & Averice of others, and its wretched Inhabitants (who through almost insuperable Difficulties, Hardships, Fatigues & Dangers at the most imminent Risque of their lives, their little all & every thing that was dear & Valuable to them, were endeavoring to secure an Asylum & a safe Retreat from threatening Penury for their tender & numerous Families with which they had removed from the lower Provinces & settled themselves in different Parts of the afore said Lands & Claims. Agreeable to the usual Mode of Colonization & Ancient equitable & long established Custom & usage of the Colonies, the Rights of Pre-Emption whenever those Lands could be rightfully & legally conveyed & disposed of after surmounting every other obstacles to their hopes, their wishes, their Expectations now unhappily find themselves in a worse & more deplorable situation than whilst living on the poor barren rented Lands in their various respective Provinces below; through Party Rage, the Multiplicity of Proprietory Claims & Claimants & the Precariousness & Uncertainty of every kinds of Property from the fore cited causes, the want of regular Administration of Justice & of a due & proper Execution & Exertion of a system of Laws & Regulations & Mode of Polity & Government adapted to their peculiar Necessities, local Circumstances & Situation & its Inhabitants, who through neighter Politicians, Courtiers nor orators, are at least a rational & Social People, inured to hardships & Fatigues & by Experience taught to despise Dangers & Difficulties, & having immigrated from almost every Province of America, brought up under & accustomed to vareous different & in many respects discordant and even contradictory Systems of Laws & Government &

Appendix II

since their being here from the want of Laws & order irritated & exasperated by ills & urged & compelled by oppressions & sufferings, & having imbided the highest & most extensive ideas of Liberty, as the only pure efficient Source of happiness & Prosperity will with difficulty submit to the being annexed to or Subjugated by (Terms Synonomous to them) any one of those Provinces , much less the being partitioned or parcelled out among them, or be prevailed on to Entail a State of Vassalage & Dependence on their Posterity or suffer themselves who might be the happiest & perhaps not the least useful Part of the American Confederacy as forming a secure extensive & Effectual Frontier & Barrier against the Incursions, Ravages, Depredations of the Western savages to be enslaved by any set of Proprietary or other claimants or arbitrarily deprived & robbed of those Land & that country to which by the Laws of Nature & of Nations they are entitled as first occupants & for the Possessions of which they have resigned their all & exposed themselves & Families to Inconveniences, Dangers & Difficulties which language itself wants word to express & describe, whilst the Rest of their Countrymen sottened by Ease, enervated by Affluence & Luxurious Plenty & accustomed to Fatigues, Hardships, Difficulties or Dangers are bravely Contending for & Exerting themselves on Behalf of a Constitutional, National, rational & Social Liberty:

We the Subscribers Inhabitants of the Country as aforesaid therefore by Lean- hereby plenarily, amply & specially delegated, interested, authorize & impowered to act & to do for us on this occasion as our Representatives, Solicitors, Agents & Attornies Humbly to represent to you, as the Guardians, Trustees & Curates, Conservators & Defences of all that is dear to us or valuable to Americans, that in our opinions no Country or People can be either rich, flourishing, happy or free (the only laudable rightful, useful, warrantable & rational Ends of Government) to enjoy the Sweets of Liberty, the Love & Desire of which is radically impressed or Self Existent with & animates & actuates every brave, generous, humane, and honest soul, and for which every American Breast at this time pants & glows with an unusual Flow of Warmth & Expectation & with redoubled Zeal and

Ardor whilst annexed to or dependent on any Province whose Seat of Government is those of Pennsylvania or Virginia four or five hundred miles distant and Separated by vast, extensive & almost impassable Tract of Mountains by Nature itself formed & pointed out as a boundary between this Country & those below it, that Justice might be both Tedious & Expensive, the Execution of the Laws dilatory & perhaps mercenary, if not arbitrary ; Redress of Grievances precarious and Slow and the Country so Situated without participating of any of the Advantages, Suffer all the Inconveniences of such a Government & be continually exposed, as we already too well know by Dear bought & fatal experience, to the Violence, Frauds, Depredations, Exactions, Oppressions of interested, ambitious, designing, insolent, avaricious, rapacious, & mercenary Men and Officers.

And pray that the Said Company be constituted declared & acnowledged a separate, distinct, and Independent Province & Government by the Title and under the Nature of - "the Providence & Government of Westsylvania" be empowered & enabled to form such Laws & Regulations & such a System of Polity & Government as is best adapted & most agreeable to the peculiar Necessities, local Circumstances & Situation thereof & its inhabitants invested with every other Power, Right, Privilege & Immunity, vested, or to be vested in the other American Colonies, be considered as a Sister Colony & the fourteenth Province of the American Confederacy: that its Boundaries Beginning at the Eastern Branch of the Ohio opposite the mouth of the Ohio opposite the mouth of the Scioto & running thence in a direct Line to the top of the Alleghany Mountains, thence with the tops of said Mountain to the Northern Limits of the Purchase made from the Indians in 1768, at the Treaty of Fort Stanwix aforesaid, thence with the said Limits to the Allegheny or Ohio River, and thence down the said River as purchased from the Indians at the aforesaid Treaty of Fort Stanwix to the Beginning.

And that for the more effectual Prevention of all future & Further Frauds and Impositions being practiced upon us, thereby all Property or other Claims or Grants heretofore, by, or to whomsoever made of

Appendix II

Lands within the aforesaid Limits of the said Province be discountenanced & Suspended to all Intent & Purposes, until approved of & Confirmed by the Legislature Body of the said Province with & under the Approbation & Sanction of the General Congress , or Grand Continental Council of State of the United American Colonies.

And your Memorialities, as by all the Ties of Duty, Interest & Honor bound as Americans, Brethren & Associates, embarked with you in the Same Arduous and glorious Cause of Liberty & Independency shall ever Pray that your Councils & Endeavors for the Common Good, may be continually attended, blessed & crowned with a never ceasing & uninterrupted Series of Success, Happiness & Prosperity.

OTHER FAMILY HISTORY-RELATED BOOKS
BY STEVEN R. BUTLER

AVAILABLE AT Amazon.com

From London to Kentucky:
The Life and Times of James Haycraft, Jr., and His Son,
Samuel Haycraft, Sr.

Miles Away from Butler:
How a DNA Test Rewrote My Family's History

www.ingramcontent.com/pod-product-compliance
Lightning Source LLC
Chambersburg PA
CBHW071304110426
42743CB00042B/1173